T0318784

Cambridge Elements ≡

Elements in Psychology and Culture
edited by
Kenneth D. Keith
University of San Diego

FEEDING, BONDING, AND THE FORMATION OF SOCIAL RELATIONSHIPS

Ethnographic Challenges to Attachment Theory and Early Childhood Interventions

Leberecht Funk, *Free University of Berlin*
Gabriel Scheidecker, *University of Zurich*
Bambi L. Chapin, *University of Maryland*
Wiebke J. Schmidt, *Osnabrück University*
Christine El Ouardani, *California State University*
Nandita Chaudhary, *University of Delhi*

CAMBRIDGE
UNIVERSITY PRESS

CAMBRIDGE
UNIVERSITY PRESS

Shaftesbury Road, Cambridge CB2 8EA, United Kingdom

One Liberty Plaza, 20th Floor, New York, NY 10006, USA

477 Williamstown Road, Port Melbourne, VIC 3207, Australia

314–321, 3rd Floor, Plot 3, Splendor Forum, Jasola District Centre, New Delhi – 110025, India

103 Penang Road, #05–06/07, Visioncrest Commercial, Singapore 238467

Cambridge University Press is part of Cambridge University Press & Assessment, a department of the University of Cambridge.

We share the University's mission to contribute to society through the pursuit of education, learning and research at the highest international levels of excellence.

www.cambridge.org
Information on this title: www.cambridge.org/9781009306270

DOI: 10.1017/9781009306300

First published 2023

A catalogue record for this publication is available from the British Library.

ISBN 978-1-009-30627-0 Paperback
ISSN 2515-3986 (online)
ISSN 2515-3943 (print)

Feeding, Bonding, and the Formation of Social Relationships

Ethnographic Challenges to Attachment Theory and Early Childhood Interventions

Elements in Psychology and Culture

DOI: 10.1017/9781009306300
First published online: July 2023

Leberecht Funk, *Free University of Berlin*

Gabriel Scheidecker, *University of Zurich*

Bambi L. Chapin, *University of Maryland*

Wiebke J. Schmidt, *Osnabrück University*

Christine El Ouardani, *California State University*

Nandita Chaudhary, *University of Delhi*

Author for correspondence: Leberecht Funk, Leberecht.Funk@fu-berlin.de

Abstract: This Element explores multifaceted linkages between feeding and relationship formation based on ethnographic case studies in Morocco, Madagascar, Sri Lanka, Taiwan, and Costa Rica. Research demonstrates that there are many culturally valued ways of feeding children, contradicting the idea of a single universally optimal feeding standard. It demonstrates further that, in many parts of the world, feeding plays a central role in bonding and relationship formation, something largely overlooked in current developmental theories. Analysis shows that feeding contributes to relationship formation through what we call proximal, transactional, and distal dimensions. This Element argues that feeding practices can lead to qualitatively distinct forms of relationships. It has important theoretical and practical implications, calling for the expansion of attachment theory to include feeding and body-centered caregiving and significant changes to global interventions currently based on "responsive feeding." This title is also available as Open Access on Cambridge Core.

Keywords: feeding, attachment theory, ethnographic research, early childhood interventions, cross-cultural comparison

ISBNs: 9781009306270 (PB), 9781009306300 (OC)
ISSNs: 2515-3986 (online), 2515-3943 (print)

Contents

1 Perspectives on Feeding and Bonding: An Introduction

Giving, receiving, and sharing food provide powerful, deeply embodied experiences of self and others. All over the world, children are fed by the people around them. Humans do not just provide breast milk to infants but continue to feed older children in varying degrees and culturally specific ways. These experiences are central in shaping children's bodies as well as their emerging social and emotional worlds. As children receive food from others upon whom their very lives depend, they have regular experiences of being related to important others. As children grow, feeding and eating continue to be embedded in social relationships, which in many cases extend to the spiritual domain. While this socio-emotional relevance is true for children and adults around the world, the particular practices and meanings of feeding interactions vary considerably across contexts. Consequently, the particular ways in which children are fed by their caregivers have significant impacts on how they become connected to the people around them.

In this Element, we draw on our individually conducted ethnographic fieldwork in Morocco, Madagascar, Sri Lanka, Taiwan, and Costa Rica to explore how feeding contributes to the formation of social relationships in early childhood and beyond. Furthermore, we show that feeding practices vary greatly across these contexts and that they are embedded in particular social conditions and cultural meanings. We argue that these multiple modes of feeding contribute in various ways to the formation of social relationships. While our findings and arguments are embedded in anthropology and cultural psychology, we also hope to reach those in other academic and applied fields who are concerned with feeding and relationship formation, adding to the current psychological and pediatric research that dominates expert understandings of childcare and development.

This psychological and psychiatric research relies overwhelmingly on Euro-American research samples, institutions, and scholars while producing universalistic theoretical claims and guiding parenting interventions around the globe (Lachman et al., 2021; Scheidecker et al., in press). Henrich and colleagues (2010, p. 3) have pointed out that "96% of psychological samples come from countries with only 12% of the world's population." They have labeled this population "WEIRD" – Western, Educated, Industrialized, Rich, and Democratic – and argued that it is different in striking ways from most of humankind. Hence, dominant developmental science discourses and interventions are rooted in Western middle-class moral assumptions and ideas about family life that do not represent the wide variety of ways that families are organized in the

West or around the world or how feeding is practiced in everyday life. In these dominant discourses, cultural variations in child-rearing practices, socialization strategies, and developmental pathways from other sociocultural settings, even though well-documented in the ethnographic record, are regularly overlooked. If they are recognized at all, they are typically pathologized (Chaudhary & Sriram, 2020). These widespread biases and gaps are found throughout the developmental sciences and their applications. As we will show in what follows, they also have strongly influenced theories of relationship formation as well as universally applied standards of feeding.

1.1 Developmental Science and Cross-Cultural Challenges

The wide range of theories and models that the science of child development has produced inform social policy and filter down to interventions and the practice of medical professionals, social workers, educators, judges, and parents. By far the most influential theory of children's socio-emotional development is attachment theory.[1] This theory posits that children's "optimal" development depends on forming a close bond with a primary caregiver – usually the mother – to whom children can return for a feeling of safety as they explore the world. Within this model, "secure attachment" is understood to be produced when a child's primary caregiver responds "sensitively" to the child's signals in a prompt, developmentally appropriate, and consistent manner. Absent a certain level of sensitive responsiveness, children are predicted to develop less-than-ideal forms of attachment – insecure, anxious or avoidant, or even disorganized ways of relating – that are believed to have lasting negative effects throughout the life course (Mesman et al., 2016).

Anthropologists and cultural psychologists have critiqued attachment theory since its earliest iterations. Margaret Mead (1954) levied one of the first critiques, responding to a World Health Organization report on the practical implications of attachment theory by John Bowlby (1951). Over the past two decades, criticism from both disciplines has intensified (e.g., Keller & Bard, 2017; LeVine & Norman, 2001; Otto & Keller, 2014; Quinn & Mageo, 2013).

---

[1] It is important to note that other theories of relationship formation have been developed within developmental science as well. Domain socialization theory, for example, offers a somewhat broader perspective on socio-emotional socialization, which includes attachment (or "protection" as it is called there) but at the same time acknowledges the existence of additional domains or fields of parent–child interactions (e.g., reciprocity, control, guided learning, group participation) in which socialization takes place (Grusec & Davidov, 2010, 2015). However, in this Element we focus our critical attention on classical attachment theory because it is still the dominant approach in the domain of socio-emotional development – on the theoretical level as well as in applied fields (see Rosabal-Coto et al., 2017).

A fundamental point these critiques make is that attachment theory rests upon cultural models derived from the Euro-American educated middle-classes, which undermines the theory's claim of universal validity (Keller, 2018; LeVine, 2014; Vicedo, 2014). Furthermore, cross-cultural research raises ethical concerns about globally implemented attachment-based interventions (Chaudhary, 2020; Rosabal-Coto et al., 2017).

In addition to the many other critiques raised by cross-cultural research, here we focus our objections on two of developmental science's claims that are central to our arguments: (1) the claim that feeding (and other body-centered care practices) is not particularly relevant for the formation of emotional bonds and (2) the claim that there is only one optimal feeding style, namely "responsive feeding." Instead, we argue that in many cultural contexts feeding and other body-centered caregiving practices are central to the formation and shaping of human bonds and that there are diverse, culturally valued ways that this may be done.[2]

1.2 Feeding and Attachment

In attachment theory, the practice of feeding has been ascribed only minor importance. Bowlby rejected secondary drive theories, including psychoanalytic theories, that assumed that children's motivation for attachment stems from the satisfaction of hunger or libidinous drives associated with the mother's breast. Instead, he insisted that mother–infant attachment is an independent psychological need (Bowlby, 1958; Cassidy, 2016; Van der Horst, 2011; Vicedo, 2014). Having cut the relationship between feeding and attachment, mainstream attachment research in the following decades rarely studied the role of feeding in caregiving relationships (Rozin, 2007).

The position that "sensitive responsiveness" is a necessary precursor to "secure attachment" between young children and their primary attachment figures has further prevented serious consideration of feeding in attachment theory. This construct foregrounds a particular, child-led, intimate, emotion-focused interaction style at the expense of body-centered care practices such as feeding. Caregivers are expected not only to attend and respond sensitively to their children's emotional expressions but also to engage in baby talk, to mirror their children's facial expressions, and to play with them frequently. In the child development literature, the focus is laid on the elicitation of

---

[2] This argument does not imply, however, that feeding is more important for bonding than sensitive responsiveness. It depends on the sociocultural context whether feeding, sensitive responsiveness, or possibly even other aspects of the social interaction assume a central role in the formation and maintenance of attachments.

psychic-emotional intimacy, which is defined in terms of a "loving, responsive, and nurturing relationship" (Morris et al., 2018, p. 2), rather than physical care and nourishment that was foregrounded by theorists in earlier times (Burman, [1994] 2017).

However, the parenting style that is defined as optimal in attachment theory is simply not a global norm or valued way of interacting in all settings, as numerous cross-cultural (Crittenden & Clausen, 2000; Keller & Bard, 2017; LeVine & Norman, 2001; Morelli et al., 2017; Otto & Keller, 2014; Quinn & Mageo, 2013) and intracultural (Kusserow, 2004; Lareau, 2003) studies have pointed out. In many of the studied groups, caregiving practices that focus on children's physical needs such as feeding, washing, holding, and carrying are foregrounded, being variously described by these culturally grounded researchers as "pediatric" (LeVine et al., 1994), "proximal" (Keller, 2007), or "body-centered" (Scheidecker, 2023).

Heidi Keller (2007), for example, has contrasted the socialization strategies and developmental pathways of children from Western urban middle-class families with those from rural farming families in various non-Western contexts. She describes urban middle-class mothers as typically engaging in a "distal" parenting style characterized by a focus on children's verbal and emotional expressions and a quasi-equal mode of interaction based on face-to-face contact and verbal interaction – a parenting style that closely resembles "sensitive responsiveness" as described in attachment theory. In rural, non-Western contexts, by contrast, Keller sees mothers tending to use a proximal parenting style that focuses more on the physical needs of children through body contact and primary care such as feeding. Rather than leading to differences in attachment security, these two parenting styles highlight different dimensions in emerging social relationships: The distal style promotes an emphasis on *psychological autonomy* while the proximal style promotes *hierarchical relatedness*. Keller's research demonstrates that body-centered care practices like feeding may play a much more central role in caregiver–child relationships in some contexts than envisioned in attachment theory. Further, it could be argued that such body-centered care practices elicit *physical-material warmth* between mothers and children and hence contribute to the development of an emotional bond between them.

Body-centered care practices are often, but not always, accompanied by "proactive caregiving," a form of caregiving that we contrast with "responsive caregiving." In proactive caregiving, rather than waiting for young children to express needs and preferences, caregivers take the lead because they know what children require. While in popular Western discourse proactive feeding might be seen as a harmful kind of force-feeding, this is neither the implication we have in mind when using this term nor reflective of the understandings of the participants in our research. Taken together, existing ethnographic evidence indicates that feeding may play a much more crucial role for bonding in many sociocultural settings across the globe than envisioned in attachment theory.

1.3 Responsive Feeding

Attachment theory's key concept of sensitive responsiveness has been particularly influential in broader cultural models of parenting, such as "attachment parenting" or "intensive parenting" (Faircloth, 2013; Lee et al., 2014), as well as in parenting interventions around the globe (Rosabal-Coto et al., 2017). The concept of responsive caregiving has been established as a globally applied parenting standard through the Nurturing Care Framework (WHO et al., 2018). Responsive caregiving has also been used to establish recommendations about optimal feeding, which are commonly labeled as "responsive feeding" (Engle & Pelto, 2011).

The fact that attachment theory is used to define and justify globally applied standards of optimal feeding appears to contradict our earlier point that feeding does not hold a prominent place in this theory. However, this paradox dissolves when distinguishing between *what* care is being provided (e.g., nourishment) and *how* that care is delivered (e.g., responsively). While attachment theorists do not consider the practice of feeding in itself as particularly relevant to attachment development, a caregiving style that is defined by sensitive responsiveness is what is seen to matter in any parent–child interaction, including feeding.

According to the principles of responsive caregiving, feeding interactions should be guided by children's signals of hunger and satiety; caregivers should follow children's lead rather than imposing their own ideas of when and what children should eat (Engle & Pelto, 2011; Pérez Escamilla et al., 2021; Vazir et al., 2013). Caregivers should sit on the same level with children, make sustained eye contact while feeding, and respond warmly to children throughout the interaction, smiling and offering praise. Caregivers should also provide finger foods to encourage early self-feeding (Aboud et al., 2009; Vazir et al., 2013). Inherent in the concept of responsive feeding is the assumption that eating is an individual, self-regulated activity in which caregivers only assume a transitory, assisting role.

Responsive caregiving and responsive feeding as allegedly optimal parenting practices have rarely been challenged directly. As a consequence of the ethnocentric bias inherent in universalized developmental theories, attachment-based interventions amount to placing the sociocultural habits of Euro-American middle-class lifestyles at the top of a hierarchy of "good parenting." Parents who deviate from these valued behaviors are viewed only in deficit terms, for example as lacking the core characteristics of a loving parent (Vicedo, 2014). This ethnocentric bias implies serious ethical challenges to parenting interventions (Lachman et al.; 2021; Morelli et al., 2018; Scheidecker et al., 2021).

Proponents of parenting interventions might argue that even if the principles of responsive feeding grew out of a particular social and historical context, those practices might still be the ones most beneficial for children's development. For example, responsive feeding interventions are justified by the scientific claim that they reduce malnutrition in children. However, according to the only available meta-analysis about responsive feeding interventions in so-called low- and middle-income countries (Bentley et al., 2011), the existing studies could not provide consistent evidence for a resulting reduction in malnutrition. Given that there is no scientific proof for the interconnections between "responsive feeding" and desired developmental outcomes, we have to conclude that responsive feeding interventions are mainly motivated by cultural values rather than facts. We believe that a basic requirement for such interventions to be effective as well as ethically sound is to root them in existing local practices, strengths, and concerns rather than denouncing them from the outset as inferior.

1.4 Approaches from Anthropology and Cultural Psychology

Approaches from anthropology and cultural psychology offer useful perspectives for understanding local feeding practices, their connection to cultural meaning systems, and the formation of social relationships in childhood and beyond. The role of feeding in social bonding, which is the focus of this Element, has not previously been examined systematically within anthropology and cultural psychology. However, close ethnographies of family interactions in a range of places have noted ways that feeding and food-giving shape affective bonds between children and their caregivers (e.g., for New Guinea, see Barlow, 2013; for India, see Chaudhary, 2004, Kakar, 1981, and Seymour, 2013; for Taiwan, see Funk, 2022; for Micronesia, see Quinn, 2013; for Ecuador, see Rae-Espinoza, 2010; for Madagascar, see Scheidecker, 2017a; for Costa Rica, see Schmidt et al., 2023b; and for Indonesia, see Seymour, 2013).

Research within the anthropology of food (for overviews, see Klein et al, 2012; Mintz & Du Bois, 2002; Tierney & Ohnuki-Tierney, 2012), which describes and analyzes social practices involving food including commensality, table manners, mealtime interactions, gender, and social differentiation marked by food, has regularly noted the significance of food in many social relationships. There is vast ethnographic evidence that food plays a crucial role in the socio-emotional lives of people in diverse sociocultural settings on both an individual and a societal level (for Amazonia, see Brightman et al., 2016 and Costa, 2017; for Southeast Asia, see Carsten, 1997 and Janowski & Kerologue, 2007; for Sri Lanka, see Chapin, 2014; for China/Taiwan, see Dos Santos, 2009 and Stafford, 1995; for New Guinea, see von Poser, 2013; and for Southern Africa, see Richards, [1932] 2004). The publications in this area that concern themselves with children tend to focus on feeding as it relates to issues of sexuality and reproduction, embodiment and subjective experience, and breast-feeding practices (e.g., Gottlieb, 2004; Hewlett, 1991; LeVine & New, 2008; Richards, [1932] 2004; Van Esterik, 2002).

Ethnography of family and daily life also contributes to understanding the cultural embeddedness of feeding. The new kinship studies led by Carsten (2000) and others directed attention at these processes, highlighting the life-worlds of women and children. Social relationships were now described by using the term "relatedness," which comprised biological kinship as well as relationships that were produced through "kinning," that is, through diverse social practices aiming at making other persons one's kin, for example feeding and other forms of caregiving. In many parts of the world, people perceive themselves as related to each other when they live together and share food and other substances (e.g., milk, food, water; see Carsten, 1995).

Significant contributions also come from the anthropology of religion and from research about human–environment connections. In what has become known as the ontological turn, anthropology increasingly recognizes that human lifeworlds are entangled in manifold ways with diverse nonhuman beings including plants, animals, landscapes, and spiritual beings (Descola, 2013; Latour, 1996; Viveiros de Castro, 1998). In the last two decades, these insights emphasize the recognition of multiple worldviews, including those that depart from the natural sciences, a belief system that itself is based in European philosophical traditions. In many, if not most societies around the world, exchanges of food play a major role in creating or maintaining quasi-social bonds to ancestors, spirits, and deities. People in many parts of the world believe that they are only able to obtain their food because they are assisted by nonhuman agents.

Our inquiry is also grounded in research on childhood and socialization, beginning with Margaret Mead (1928, 1930), Ruth Benedict (1934), and others in the so-called Culture and Personality school and continuing through the comparative Six Cultures studies led by the Whitings (Whiting & Whiting

1975) and others who followed. An important trailblazer was the anthropologist Robert LeVine who has written on the entanglements between culture, socialization practices, parenting, and child development (LeVine et al., 1994; LeVine & LeVine, 1966; LeVine & LeVine, 2016). We build on this century-long effort to examine how child-rearing practices vary across cultures and understand how these interactions shape children in culturally distinct ways. The methods we use grow out of this tradition, with its focus on close observations of everyday life in particular places. We also share with studies of childhood (e.g., Hardman, 1973; Prout & James, 1997; Schildkrout, 1978) a recognition that children are active participants in these processes, exercising agency in their interactions, pursuing their own goals, and assembling their own understandings of themselves and the world around them.

1.5 An Element on Feeding across Cultures

The intention of this Element is to use close ethnography of how children are fed in particular places to examine the connections between feeding practices and the formation of social bonds in early childhood and beyond. The contributors to this Element are sociocultural anthropologists and cultural psychologists from Germany, the United States, and India who have carried out extensive long-term ethnographic field research in rural and urban settings in diverse regions across the globe focusing on issues of childhood and socialization. In each of the settings, we have documented how affective bonds between caregivers and young children are created and maintained through feeding practices like breastfeeding, hand-feeding, spoon-feeding, food-giving, and self-feeding. By presenting these ethnographic insights, we call for a revision of theories on human development to recognize the connection between feeding and the formation of social bonds as well as the diverse and valued ways that this may be done across the globe.

How we perceive the world is strongly influenced by the cultural models we have acquired during our own socialization in India, Germany, and the United States, as is our framing of what is interesting or notable about the settings in which we work. When writing about the people in our research settings in Morocco, Madagascar, Sri Lanka, Taiwan, and Costa Rica, the focus of our attention is inevitably directed by the values and norms of our own upbringing and by the constructs we use in our academic discourses. We strive to be mindful of that in this Element, making it clear from which perspectives we write and how we analyze what people say and do in our field sites. This approach is central to the methods of ethnography and the goals of our analysis, as we work to call into question the universal validity of attachment theory and responsive feeding. Our discussion of the commonalities and differences in feeding practices in our research sites aims to develop a plural understanding of how culturally specific feeding relationships are endowed with diverse cultural meanings.

In what follows, we present descriptions of feeding practices that play an important role in the formation of social relationships in five sociocultural settings. Our ethnographic examples stretch over three continents and cover geographically distinct areas with different ecological environments, historical and political entanglements, socioeconomic organizations, and cultural beliefs and practices. One research site is located in a big city (San José, Costa Rica), while the others are situated in rural settings – two that are close to major cities (Douar Tahtani in Morocco and Villigama in Sri Lanka), one that is in a remote and sparsely populated area (Menamaty in Madagascar), and one on a formerly isolated island (Lanyu in Taiwan). In these snapshots of daily life in particular places, we cannot capture the full range of practices or experiences in these communities or the ongoing changes that are part of all communities. Nevertheless, these observations allow us to see how much wider the possibilities are for meanings, values, and practices than is typically envisioned by current developmental science.

The examples we present are ordered moving eastward around the world: In Section 2, Christine El Ouardani demonstrates how feeding practices, the larger sensorium of the family gathering, and affect-laden interactions with extended kin during a typical mealtime in rural Morocco serve to inculcate a sense of belonging and attachment not only to the mother but to the larger extended family. In Section 3, Gabriel Scheidecker describes practices of breastfeeding, spoon-feeding, and the provision of food as a central form of care in intergenerational relationships among the Bara pastoralists of Madagascar. He argues that through these practices children acquire a model of hierarchical relationships that is characterized by the transfer of life force in exchange for subordination and obedience. In Section 4, Bambi L. Chapin describes how hand-feeding children in a Sinhala-speaking village in central Sri Lankan grows out of valued cultural models of hierarchy, which children in turn assemble internally through these embodied, emotionally salient experiences with important others. In Section 5, Leberecht Funk argues that the socialization goal for Tao caregivers in Taiwan consists in the physical survival of the bodily selves of children who are in danger of losing their souls due to the evildoings of malicious spirits. Children obtain ancestral protection by following the instructions of elders and by being provided with nourishing food that makes their bodily selves strong and resilient against supernatural harms. Finally, in Section 6, Wiebke J. Schmidt explores how the growing popularity of attachment theory among the urban middle-class in Costa Rica has influenced breastfeeding and other early childhood feeding practices to promote children's autonomy, while feeding also still promotes more traditional ideas about connecting to family. Following these ethnographic examples, we discuss salient themes and differences between each of the pieces and examine the implications of our findings for global feeding intervention programs promoted by international development projects.

2 Forming Kin Attachments during Mealtimes in Rural Morocco

In Morocco, as in most of the world, food plays a critical role in family life.[3] In media and everyday discourse, childhood memories of a mother's cooking and of gathering with family around the table are often nostalgically invoked and idealized. In conducting ethnographic fieldwork in a Moroccan village that I call Douar Tahtani from 2006 to 2008, I also observed an intense informal sociality during mealtimes, in which children were often central participants. Here, I want to consider how participation in mealtimes – both in interactions with kin and in the larger sensorium that the setting creates – structures not only attachment to their mothers but also a sense of belonging, kinship, and attachment to the larger extended family. I examine one typical mealtime interaction in particular and focus on three children under the age of five, focusing on feeding interactions between the children and their mothers, their interactions with other kin during these long meals, and the sensory experiences that the environment might create for these children. I suggest that the extended mealtime settings that children participate in several times a day may cultivate and reinforce attachments to multiple caregivers and the larger kin group. Mealtimes are thus central to kin formation, in part through feeding practices but also through other affect-laden physical and verbal interactions that occur during mealtimes. The fieldwork on which this Element is based included two years of intensive participant observation resulting in more than 1,000 pages of fieldnotes, 75 semi-structured interviews, and 10 hours of video recordings of mealtimes across 3 different households, all of which were conducted in the Moroccan dialect of Arabic. In all, I worked closely with approximately 20 adults and 40 children ranging from newborns to 15-year-olds and casually knew more than 100 adults and children in this village.

---

[3] The ethnographic research and original analysis presented in this section was conducted by Christine El Ouardani, one of the coauthors of this Element. This research was funded by the Fulbright-Hays Program, the National Science Foundation, the H. F. Guggenheim Foundation, and the American Institute for Maghrib Studies.

2.1 Family and Everyday Life in Douar Tahtani

Douar Tahtani is an Arabic-speaking Moroccan village located near the city of Fez in the foothills of the Rif mountains. This patrilocal agricultural community consists of about 10,000 people, half of whom are under the age of 18. Families grow and harvest wheat, olives, peas, and fava beans, and men supplement this income with construction work in the city or by working on other people's land. Women do most of the intensive housework and child-rearing, including food preparation, washing laundry by hand, and tending to the animals that live in the family compound. This community is among the poorest rural communities in Morocco, although recent investments in electricity, roads, running water, and now local schools and internet connectivity have improved the economic outlook of many families and especially their children, who have new oppor-tunities for education and employment in local development projects.

Families tend to be large in Douar Tahtani and many people live in extended family households consisting of married brothers and their wives and children, along with their parents and unmarried sisters. Most married couples had between four and ten children, and having many children in this context is highly valued as a source of pleasure and abundance. Both patriarchal authority and filial piety are valorized in this context, and children are expected to submit to and honor their parents, especially their fathers. At the same time, Tahtanis encourage their children to demonstrate *ssahha* – strength, fortitude, and independence – as an attribute of their rural identity and in order to be able to help defend and work hard for their families. Interactions between children and their kin thus often contain a tension between these ideals of submission and strength/independence. For example, corporal discipline is a common practice with children, and yet there are often episodes of affection and play incorporated into these otherwise painful and angry interactions, which I argue elsewhere encourage children both to submit to rightful kin authority and to resist this authority and develop an ability to defend themselves (El Ouardani, 2018). Similar to the interactions that Briggs (1998) describes between children and their adult kin, these interactions cultivate a sense of ambivalence toward kin authority and encourage a child's agency while also reinforcing the affectionate bonds between kin even in the face of the imposition of authority. Children are generally given a great deal of independence and wander the village freely, playing with their peers and older children, with little direct oversight from their parents. They are valued for the household and agricultural labor they contribute and the important social roles they play in running errands, managing conflict with other families, and gathering news and information from others in the village. Young children are generally shown a great deal of affection and care by their kin and neighbors (El Ouardani, 2014).

2.2 Eating and Mealtimes

During my fieldwork, eating and mealtimes were a central social activity in households in Douar Tahtani. There were four meals served every day. Breakfast (*iftar*) was served mid-morning once the morning agricultural work was done. Lunch (*lghdda*) was the main meal and was eaten in the early-to-mid afternoon. It often consisted of a vegetable stew with a little bit of meat (*tajin*), served with homemade bread. The early evening tea (*qasqrote*) was served with bread and condiments and often filtered into the final meal of the day (*lAsha*), which might consist of another *tajin* or some soup. During each of these meals, the entire family gathered, including children and adults from the household who are not otherwise occupied, possibly along with family members from other house-holds. During these extended interactions (usually lasting more than an hour), Tahtanis ate, talked, laughed, and sometimes argued about the goings on in the household and in the larger community. The mood was often lively and talkative but also informal and relaxed. These meals were the central activity where families came together to spend time with each other and enact kinship. The women and older girls in the household all participated in the meal preparation, often on a rotating schedule (*nouba*) to ensure equity across female household labor.

2.3 Feeding Young Children

Babies and infants were usually at least partially breastfed from birth, although the length of time varied greatly depending on the mother, child, and birth order. Babies were most often nursed exclusively by their mothers, although milk-sharing between women still existed in cases when a mother had a low supply of milk or even just casually to signify or form stronger social or kin ties. Sharing milk created a kin bond between the baby and the nursing woman, known as a milk mother (*mmee mn rdaA*). The milk child then became a full sibling to her children, creating an incest taboo between the child and the woman and her children, although this bond was not as strong as blood ties and did not confer inheritance rights, for example. Milk kinship was very common in Douar Tahtani in the past but was practiced much less during the time of my fieldwork, with the advent of formula and the decrease in the length of time a child is breastfed. Women and men often cited two years as the ideal amount of time for a child to be breastfed, based on Islamic recommendations. However, most women did not breastfeed for this long because of the significant amount of house and agricultural work that they need to attend to, which makes it difficult to exclusively breastfeed, as well as physical discomfort and difficulties that especially younger mothers seem to have with breastfeeding. Formula was available to infants, although the cost was often prohibitive to families.

Babies were often also given boiled milk and sweetened tea and were encouraged to start eating solid foods several months after birth.

Babies and young children were nursed and fed by hand at the table with their mother and other kin. As they became older and more disruptive, they were then sent to eat separately with other children, from a separate plate, where they learned to feed themselves – usually between the ages of two and three. Adults felt that children were dirty and did not want them to eat directly from the same shared plate, although they were usually fed at the same time and in the same room as their adult kin in the evenings. At lunch, children sometimes ate outside before the adult meal. In general, there was a great deal of informality that infused mealtimes, with children coming in and out of the room where the adults eat. Children were often fed by hand by multiple kin, especially by mothers, aunts, and grandmothers. Children were never forced to eat foods they disliked, nor were they required to eat at specific times. If a child was hungry for a snack outside of mealtimes, they were freely given food if it was available.

2.4 Cultivating Kinship and Belonging during Mealtimes

In Douar Tahtani, feeding practices created kinship bonds, as in the example of the milk mother. In the rest of this section, I examine how the gathering of the extended family for mealtimes and the emotional tone of these interactions served to cultivate feelings of belonging, warmth, and affection toward the kin group throughout the course of childhood. I describe one very typical thirty-five-minute gathering that I videorecorded in 2008, in order to focus on the interactional details that create a specific emotional and sensory experience for the child (Figure 1).

Figure 1 A Tahtani family gathered for the afternoon meal. © Christine El Ouardani

In this scene, members of the household had gathered in the early evening for the *qasqrote* – the afternoon tea that precedes the evening meal. The adults present included one of the married sons in the household, his unmarried brother, two unmarried sisters, his sister-in-law, his cousin visiting from the city, and me, later to be joined by the married son's wife and mother. All five children who lived in the household were present, as well as several cousins of these children who came in and out of the room until the food was served. The sharing of food demarcates who belongs to a household, and thus the neighbor cousins left when the food was served, as they were not a direct part of the household that shared labor and resources.

We were all seated on the ground, sitting closely next to one another against the walls of the well-lit room, moving toward the center of the room once the food was served at the table in the center of the room. There were pillows, blankets, and sheepskins for comfort and warmth. Multiple conversations were occurring and the adults in the room were talking animatedly about the events of the day – who visited whom, the price of items at the market, reflections on the housework and behavior of the children, and general gossip about other villagers. Although children were not directly involved in these conversations, they often listened intently and quietly to what their kin were saying when not engaged in other activities. The two adult brothers were trying to feed milk in a bottle to a young lamb that they found who had been abandoned by its mother, and most of the children in the room gathered around, observing the lamb and the attempts to save it. The emotional tone of the room was lively, warm, and informal, as both the adults and children were relaxing after a long day of hard work and play in the fields and at home.

In what follows, I focus on the experiences of the three youngest children in the room in order to reflect on how mealtimes and feeding practices reinforced close bonds between mothers and their children, but also between children and other members of the extended family, and the sense of the extended family household as a whole.

2.4.1 Sami

At eighteen months old, Sami was the youngest child at the meal and the youngest of his four siblings. During this meal, as during many meals, he mostly stayed next to his mother, observing what was going on in the room from the security of her lap. He hugged her, and she kissed and cuddled him throughout the interaction.

Sami repeatedly gazed at his mother's face, tried to get her attention when she looked away from him (*mama mama*), and whined when she briefly got up and went to the other room. His whining was pretty constant (*mama mama*), perhaps because he was hungry. However, he waited somewhat patiently on her lap for the bread to come. Once the food was placed on the table for the larger group (bread with jam and butter), he became more insistent, even hitting her in the face several times to get her attention for some bread. She quickly reached over and broke off some of the bread for him, dipped it in the jam, fed him a bite, and then handed the rest to him to eat for himself. As soon as he had eaten the piece, he started whining again for more food, and she handed him a glass of sweetened tea and another piece of bread. He then sat next to her quietly eating and watching his uncles and cousins trying to feed the lamb. Sami then went back to his mother's lap and pulled at her shirt, requesting to be nursed, although his mother did not comply perhaps because I was videotaping. Sami clearly saw his mother as the main way to get fed. He did not dare to grab directly from the table but rather waited for her to give him his food. After he had finished eating, he crawled back onto his mother's lap and resumed trying to get her attention while she was engaged in talking with others, until she finally carried him out of the room to put him to sleep in their shared room across the courtyard.

2.4.2 Zineb

Sami's two-and-a-half-year-old sister Zineb was much more physically and socially engaged with her other kin at the meal, although she did go to her mother for food once it was served. She was initially focused on observing her uncle feeding the lamb, along with her older brothers and other cousins, and talking with her brothers and aunt. She then wandered over to her mother and sat next to her, although her little brother pushed her out the way when she tried to climb onto her lap. Her mother also shooed her away, so she stood next to her mother, watching the other kids playing with a flashlight, and tried to get her mother's attention to show her what was going on. Zineb sat quietly next to her mother for some time and then wandered over to her adult male cousin who cuddled her for a while on his lap, while she continued to watch her uncle feeding the lamb. Once the food was served, Zineb wandered over to her aunt and sat next to her, before returning to her mother's side. Zineb's mother handed her bread and jam, and she stood quietly next to her, eating, until she was done, at which point she placed the bread back in her mother's hand. Zineb continued to stand next to her mother until her beloved grandmother came in to sit down and eat, at which point Zineb walked over to her to sit on her lap. They had a close bond, as her grandmother took over many of her mother's caretaking duties, including feeding, when Zineb's younger brother was born a year after her own birth. Zineb and her grandmother often slept next to each other at night, and Zineb took a lot of comfort in her presence.

2.4.3 Mounir

Mounir, Zineb and Sami's cousin and the only son of the married brother present at this meal, was three years old in this video and was also quite engaged with multiple kin during mealtime. He was initially engaged in helping his father feed the young lamb they found and tried to play with it, imitating the noises that sheep make. He tried to engage playfully with his adult male cousin and aunt and then took some sunflower seeds from his cousin to snack on. He became fascinated with playing with a flashlight that his cousin gave him and then returned to observing the care of the lamb for an extended period of time. When his mother, who had cooked the food for the evening, came in and sat down, he eventually made his way to her side. This very active boy, who spent most of his day outside engaged in intense play, was quite tired at this point and lay down with his head in his mother's lap, watching his kin as they talked. His mother handed him a piece of bread and some sweetened tea and he sat quietly next to her and ate.

2.5 Analysis and Conclusion

Although all of these children, to some extent, looked to their mothers for food and comfort during mealtimes, we see that as they progressively grew older, their mealtime interactions with kin expanded and they explored relationships with these adult kin, as well as other children and even animals who are part of the household, during these times. Young Sami almost exclusively focused on his mother, while also taking in the lively, affection-ate talk going on around him and watching what his siblings and cousins were doing from his mother's lap. Although Zineb still relied on her mother for food and nourishment (although at other times her grandmother and aunts fed her, as well) she sought out affection from other kin – especially her older cousin and her grandmother. She delighted in the activities of the group – the feeding of the lamb and the novelty of the flashlight. Mounir was the most fully engaged with the larger group – actively delighting in participating in feeding the lamb and playing with the flashlight, while also returning to mom for nourishment and rest.

We thus see in this rural Moroccan context young children experienced their mothers as a source of nourishment and comfort when being fed. This experi-ence was often extended to grandmothers and aunts, especially amongst children who have younger siblings, widening the sphere of kin who can act like mothers and feed children. Beyond the provision of food, however, mealtime served as an important space for children to develop relationships to extended kin both within and outside of the household and as a contained space in which they developed a sense of the family as a place of safety and well-being. Mealtime was also a place where authority was upheld and yet simultaneously contested, as I explore in other work. It was a space with multiple emotional tones and multi-sensorial experience – the affectionate (and sometimes rough) touch of multiple kin members; the lively, playful, and warm (although at other times angry) talk in the room; the soft blankets, warm lighting, and smell and taste of the food. Through individual interactions during these multiple, daily interactions, children came to *feel* as part of this kin group. The juxtaposition of the feeling of being fed with these other sensory experiences created important associations between belonging to a family and being fed.

3 From Breast Milk to Ancestral Blessings: Feeding through the Life Course in a Pastoralist Community of Madagascar

Menamaty is a rural community of a dozen villages in the region of Ihorombe in southern Madagascar where I conducted fifteen months of ethnographic research on childhood between 2009 and 2015 (Scheidecker, 2017a).[4] With few exceptions, the villagers self-identified as Bara pastoralists and maintained a subsistence lifestyle. They engaged in wet rice cultivation and grew some other crops, including casava. Agriculture was limited by the semi-arid climate, with an eight-month dry season, and villagers did not see it as a priority. They considered raising zebu cattle based on the vast grass savannahs in the area as the main economic activity that could bring wealth and prestige. The wealthiest person among the roughly 350 inhabitants of the village, where I did most of my research, owned about 600 heads of cattle, while others had only a couple, often due to cattle raiding (Scheidecker, 2014, 2017b). This considerable inequality, however, did not at all affect the living conditions. Houses, the quality of clothes, and the foods consumed were similar across the population and did not reveal anything about the wealth of their owners.

In contrast to agriculturalists in Madagascar, Bara pastoralists settled in remote, sparsely populated areas that were favorable for cattle raising, and they were rather resistant to "foreign ways of life" (*fomban'bazaha*). The villages of Menamaty were not connected to the road system of Madagascar or to the electricity grid or phone network. Colonial and more recent efforts to Christianize the population and establish schooling in the region proved untenable. Aside from a few migrants from other regions of Madagascar, the

---

[4] The ethnographic research and original analysis presented in this section was conducted by Gabriel Scheidecker, one of the coauthors of this Element. His research was funded by the German Research Foundation (DFG). Etienne Tsiavela and Dadah Garcon Sambo assisted in data collection and interpretation.

villagers did not consider themselves Christian. Instead, their religious practices and beliefs were centered on ancestral spirits. Education in Menamaty
was informal during the period of data collection. The village population
spoke exclusively Malagasy, a Malayo-Polynesian language that is used all
over Madagascar.

3.1 Food, Relationships, and Emotions

Rice was clearly the staple food, usually consumed at the two daily meals, one in
the morning and the main meal in the evening. Only when the stock of rice was
exhausted before the next harvest was it replaced by manioc, which villagers
considered an inferior food. The rice meal was sometimes accompanied by one
small bowl of egg, peanuts, river fish, beans, honey, locusts, or manioc leaves,
depending on the current availability. Frequently, meals consisted solely of rice.
Beef was consumed irregularly as cattle were slaughtered only on occasion of
a sacrifice. Vegetables and fruit were not part of the regular diet, and salt was the
only spice used.

This limited variety of food was not a result of a lack of resources – no family in
the region suffered from food scarcity at the time of my research.[5] Rather, the
limit was due to an emphasis on the nutritional value of specific foods. Food
variety and the pleasure or conviviality extended meals could bring along were
not commonly valued. Meals were eaten hastily and silently in small groups of
family members or alone, separated by gender and hidden behind closed doors,
which otherwise remained open during the day. In the beginning of my fieldwork,
I tried to be polite by praising the food I received – until my field assistant told me
that this was awkward as I could appear as a "gourmand," as somebody who
indulges too much in eating. In fact, to express any desire for food was considered
undignified, especially for men.

Potential desires for food were further restricted by a large number of food
taboos, some shared by all, some inherited from the parents, some individually
imposed in the context of healing rituals. As a result, most of the wild animals,
roots, or fruits were taboo for a considerable proportion of the villagers.
Guineafowls, for example, were forbidden for most villagers, as a consequence
of which they had to be cooked and eaten in the forest. Finally, it was considered
a sign of extreme poverty to collect and hunt for food eagerly, since it would
indicate a lack of rice. Rice and beef – and breast milk for infants – were
considered to be the only truly nourishing foods.

---

[5] As of writing, the region is now affected by the current drought in the south of Madagascar,
leading to food scarcity.

Eating as a potential occasion for conviviality was equally de-emphasized. During festive events which could last for several days, the participants withdrew temporarily into their houses for eating. Typically, the available food during such festivities was even less varied than usual because nobody had time or motivation to provide anything else than rice or – if a sacrifice was involved – beef. The only exception was the possession ritual *bilo*, which climaxes in feasting by the possessed individuals in front of a starving audience. The possessed state is generally expressed by turning behavioral norms on their head. When the feast and state of possession were terminated, the "dispossessed" individuals usually covered their face and left the scene as quickly as possible. To take in food was, under normal circumstances, almost as embarrassing as discharging it. Enjoyment and conviviality appeared to be confined to drinking – beer, rum, and soft drinks – which were only consumed during celebrations.

Nevertheless, food was highly socially significant to the people of Menamaty; this was based on the transfer of food rather than on the pleasure or sociability of eating. The villagers shared an understanding of food as the prime material manifestation of "life force" (*ay*) or "blessing" (*fitahia*) that parents and ancestors transfer to their descendants. The life of individuals was believed to depend existentially on a constant influx of life force from the previous generation, be it through the daily provision of food or the blessing needed to keep cattle, land, and humans fertile and healthy.

The intergenerational transfer of food and blessing was emphasized in ceremonial as well as mundane social interaction. Since cattle were only slaughtered for the purpose of a sacrifice to the ancestors, their flesh was explicitly consumed as a material manifestation of ancestral blessing. Although each nuclear family cultivated their own rice, they were obliged to perform the ritual of the "first fruit" (*loha voly*) before any harvest was released for consumption. In this ritual, a symbolic share of the harvest is presented to the head of the lineage who offers it to the ancestors, receives their blessing, eats from it himself, and then releases the rest of the harvest (see Elli, 1993, p. 86; Faublée, 1954, p. 14; Huntington, 1988, p. 57). The idea that food or the means to produce it originates from the elders and previous generations is underlined in miniature at every meal. Each bowl of food could only be touched after the elder had taken at least a spoonful. The end of the meal also followed this temporal rule, with the eldest finishing first and the youngest last. If younger ones wanted to stop eating before the elders, they were expected to apologize by lifting the shared eating bowl with both hands. During my fieldwork, these rules were always rigorously observed.

While the transfer of food and vitality from the older to the younger is performed on a daily basis and in a ritualized manner, its affective force manifests itself most clearly if this normalcy is interrupted. If individuals fail to obey elders or violate the norms imposed by the ancestors, they experience *havoa*, a life-threatening loss of life force. Among many who reported similar experiences, one nineteen-year-old shared this:

> When I was still married, I lived in the village of my wife. My father did not agree and finally expelled me. Since then I harvested only little rice, and I realized that I have been hit by *havoa*. Later I also became ill: I got a fever, headache, and a wound on my leg without an obvious reason so that I could barely walk. At that time, I was angry at my father, sad to have lost my siblings, and scared that the ancestors would fetch me. Finally, I begged my father to perform a sacrifice . . . Since then I stay with him again.

Thus, the gift of food and, by extension, of life force, which has to be reciprocated by obedience and subordination, is at the center of hierarchical relationships in Menamaty. Feeding practices and other care practices in early childhood may shed a light on how these emotional and social dynamics around food are acquired.

3.2 Feeding and Other Care Practices in Infancy

Mothers and others cared for infants in a distinctly body-centered manner; that is, they focused on children's physical needs and well-being. As indicated by more than 800 spot observations, caregivers provided almost constant body contact, while almost never engaging in face-to-face contact, play, or emotionally stimulating interactions with infants. Children did have ample experiences of such distal stimulating interactions; however, this was mainly in egalitarian relationships with similar-aged siblings or cousins (see Scheidecker, 2023). According to seventy-one extensive interviews about child-rearing, the primary goals of mothers and other caregivers were children's rapid physical growth and motor development, as well as resistance to diseases. The most important behavioral goal for caregivers was to keep the child in a calm state, which they characterized as having a "clear heart" (*mazava fo*) or a "disengaged heart" (*afa-po*).

My interview partners unanimously described breastfeeding as a crucial care practice that was most effective in achieving all of these developmental and behavioral goals. One mother of six children explained: "You breastfeed an infant as often as possible because it grows fastest through the mother's milk – especially when the mother's breast milk is 'hot' (*mafana ronono*). When that's the case, it grows really fast and without any problems." The concept of hot or cold breastmilk, which caregivers frequently raised to explain the variation in children's physical growth, refers to the amount of life force in the milk. Furthermore, caregivers pointed to breastfeeding as the single most effective way to soothe children and keep them in a calm state. As a twelve-year-old babysitter described, "the child only cries when she wants to be breastfed, while her mother is occupied and leaves her with me. When she is then breastfed, she immediately stops crying and then starts to play with a bottle." My observations confirmed these descriptions: Mothers breastfed their children amply, usually several times an hour. To offer the breast was typically the first thing mothers did when children appeared fussy or simply a bit unsettled. Interestingly, mothers rarely focused visually on the child while nursing. Rather, their visual attention was devoted to other activities such as working or chatting with adult companions, even while the child began or stopped drinking. Breastfeeding was not conceptualized as an emotionally intimate interaction but rather as the transmission of a powerful substance from the mother to the child.

Breastfeeding also played a crucial role in the relationship between mothers and children. Mothers described breastfeeding as a practice that distinguishes them from all other caregivers. Consequently, the special relationship to the child ends with weaning, as a mother of four pointed out: "There will be little contact between the two of us, once I stop breastfeeding my child. Maybe by then my other children will have a close relationship with him because he will be 'grown up'. He will play a lot with his friends by then." In case parents separated while their child was still being breastfed, the child remained with the mother until weaning, whereupon the father could claim the child according to patrilocal principles. While some mothers talked about this physical distance from the child upon weaning in neutral terms, especially if another child was on the way, others expressed some sadness. A few older mothers told me that they had nursed their last child considerably longer than the others, until the age of seven in one case, in order to keep close contact.

3.3 Ontogenetic Changes in Feeding Practices

According to spot observations, the children of Menamaty experienced a dramatic reduction in bodily contact during their first three years, from nearly 80 percent of the time in infancy to less than 5 percent for two-year-olds (for details, see Scheidecker, 2023). In fact, toddlers were expected to avoid all physical contact with parents and other adults and even to keep a respectful distance from them. An important milestone in this rapid decline of proximal care was weaning, which most children experienced at the end of the second year (21.4 months on average) in quite an abrupt manner, for example when a mother would put a spicy substance on her nipples or separate herself from her child for several weeks.

Similar observations in many other rural communities have been interpreted as "parental rejection" (Ritchie & Ritchie, 1979, p. 57), "disindulgence" (Levy, 1978, p. 226), and "toddler rejection" (Lancy, 2007, p. 276). However, my interlocutors found the suggestion that toddlers experience a hurtful rejection to be implausible. For them, the central dimension of hierarchical relationships – the intergenerational transmission of life force – continues throughout one's entire life, while only the modes of transmission change: from constant body contact and breastfeeding in infancy to the provision of food in childhood to rituals of blessing and healing throughout adulthood. Based on my observations, I argue that children in Menamaty did indeed have ample opportunities to experience feeding as the core of care and of hierarchical relationships throughout the life course.

From birth until well into the second year of life, children experienced breastfeeding as the first, and often the only, form of maternal attention when they were distressed or upon reunion. While breastfeeding in infancy is embedded in the experience of continuous bodily care, it increasingly crystallizes as the core of care in the second year of life, since mothers begin to refrain from other forms of body contact once children become mobile. A typical observation was that a one-year-old toddler would approach the mother, drink immediately, and, as soon as they had enough milk, quickly rejoin their peers.

At the age of weaning, other ways of feeding were already well established: Spoon-feeding, mostly of rice porridge, was introduced in early infancy (around three months). In contrast to breastfeeding, children frequently experienced spoon-feeding with caregivers other than the mother, mostly older siblings, aunts, or grandmothers, allowing children to associate the feeding experience with female caregivers more generally. At around six months, children started to eat "finger foods" such as a piece of manioc or fish, and most one-year-olds could be seen eating rice with a spoon. All two-year-old children ate entirely without any help. Correspondingly, caregivers frequently mentioned early self-feeding as an important developmental goal, along with walking, getting dressed or undressed, washing the face, or defecating. A grandmother explained:

> When we eat, I give her [grandchild, around one year old] a small plate and tell her "Take your spoon in your hand, eat with it." Then when she eats, a lot of the rice falls on the floor and only some goes into her mouth. I then say again, "Eat with the spoon so that you become 'reasonable' (*mahitsy*)." In this way, she gradually gets used to everything new.

Fostering early self-feeding is in line with the approach outlined in Section 3.1, which prioritizes food provision over the social interaction during feeding.

Through this channeling of continuous body-centered care to nursing and intermittent feeding, children may experience food provision not just as a residue of care but rather as an act that comes to epitomize care and their bond to mothers and other caregivers. According to the spot observations, toddlers most often approached their mothers on the occasion of a meal or to receive food. Furthermore, toddlers often held a piece of food for extended periods in their hand while playing with their peers, occasionally putting it into the mouth. These pieces of food may have a similar function for the children in Menamaty as cuddly toys have for children in other contexts – they may provide some kind of comfort while the caregiver is absent, although through food rather than cuddling. While I am unable to further substantiate this interpretation for toddlers, older children and adults expressed in various interviews that feeding, in particular its nourishing, life-sustaining function, is a crucial dimension of their relationship to parents and ancestors.

Once children reach around four or five years of age, they are taught that food and physical well-being is not an unconditional gift. From this age onward, children are expected to respect and obey their elders in return. To enforce these expectations, and to instill a kind of moral "fear" (*tahotsy*), disobedient children could be punished by beatings or food deprivation (for details, see Röttger-Rössler et al., 2013; Röttger-Rössler et al., 2015). All children I interviewed were able to recall such an experience. A fourteen-year-old boy told me: "I once refused to collect firewood because I felt exhausted. My father did it himself and said thereafter, 'You exist only through me. If you don't help, you won't get to eat.' Only in the evening, he called me to have dinner. But now I refused to eat because my 'stomach felt dirty' (*maloto troky*)."

Such a marked experience of a threat or physical discomfort inflicted by parents highlights that the food children normally receive on a daily basis cannot be taken for granted but rather depends on their respectful and obedient behavior. Furthermore, these sanctioning episodes underline an ideology according to which fathers and the patriline are the true source of food, which may not occur naturally to children as they usually receive food from mothers and female caregivers. Crucially, these lessons are associated with intensive feelings. The term *maloto troky* in the episode above, and a dozen similar stomach metaphors, refers to a kind of suppressed anger and physical malaise centered in the stomach, which my interview partners frequently used to describe their feelings in response to a conflict with parents or elders (for more details, see Scheidecker, 2020). In addition, children typically experienced intense fear in the face of physical punishment. Thus, through such disciplining practices, children may learn to associate a disturbance in their relationship to parents with feelings of malaise and fears about their physical well-being.

From adolescence on, the direct provision of food or punishment through parents begins to cease. At this age, ancestral spirits – often of a grandparent or even the father if he died early – are believed to assume these roles through providing or withholding life force. There are several ways in which a supernatural extension of earlier experiences with corporeal caregivers can become tangible. An individual may become ill and, if combined with some norm violation, may tend to interpret it as the onset of *havoa*, a life-threatening disease inflicted by the ancestors. Such an individual may also be sent to the "diviner" (*ombiasy*) who may diagnose *havoa* based on an oracle, as in the *havoa*-episode quoted in Section 3.1. A disobeying individual may also be expelled from their lineage, which cuts them off from patrilineal blessing. The physical discomfort and fear may be countered by an apology to the parents and sacrifice to ancestors in order to regain their blessing.

3.4 Conclusion

In Menamaty, I have argued, feeding in the sense of providing food and sustenance is elaborated as the central dimension of parent–child and other intergenerational relationships. Children and even adults are considered unable to live and remain healthy without a continuous influx of food or life force from their parents and ancestors. The affective foundation of these food-based relationships is most clearly expressed (and probably felt) when individuals fear becoming physically weak or ill or even dying in consequence of a conflict with their parents or other ancestors resulting from disobedience or norm violations.

Children acquire such a food-focused bond to their parents and other caregivers in the context of a body-centered caregiving style in the first year of life that becomes increasingly centered around nursing and other forms of feeding from the second year on. Later in childhood, the vital significance of this transfer is accentuated through viscerally and emotionally intense experiences of food deprivation and other forms of physical punishment in consequence of disobedience. From adolescence on, these concrete experiences are embedded in a model of supernatural blessing and punishment that can be navigated by moral behavior and rituals of sacrifice. The ontogenetic transitions from nursing, to spoon-feeding, to food provision and deprivation, and to blessing and cursing go along with a social expansion of their relational model from mothers to other caregivers to fathers and ancestral spirits. Interestingly, the more abstract roles and concepts that children acquire later are represented as more fundamental, which is perhaps best expressed in an idiom that every child knows: *Ray aman-dreny Zagnahary hita masu!* – "Fathers and mothers are visible gods!"

4 Learning about Hierarchy through Hand-Feeding in Sri Lanka

When I asked people in the Sinhala village I call Viligama what the most important thing parents must do for their children, they told me that parents must provide.[6] They must provide clothing, schooling, advice, and eventually see that their children are set up with marriages and incomes. In conducting participant observation and interviewing over the past two decades with women and children in Sri Lanka, as well as with fathers and other family members, teachers, and healthcare workers, this emphasis on a parent's primary obligation as providing for their children came up again and again, folding under it other parenting tasks and decisions. When I asked parents how they decided how many children to have, for instance, they regularly told me that, while everyone loves children, parents should not have more than they can be sure to provide for, a sentiment borne out in national average family sizes of two to three children and high indicators of health and education.

Food was the most concrete, daily, and emblematic example of what parents provide. In interviews, it is what parents returned to again and again in discussing how to raise children. Moreover, I have come to see that the particular *ways* that caregivers provide food to children demonstrate even more about these relationships and how children learn to participate in them.

In what follows, I describe daily interactions in which children were fed by hand by affectionate mothers and other caregivers who were confident about what their children needed. As they made little balls of rice and curry with their fingers and popped them into their children's waiting mouths, children's cooperation was needed but not their verbal participation or expression of preferences. What I came to see was that, as children participated in these interactions shaped by older people's understandings about children and proper ways of relating, children were taking in more than just food. Through regular, embodied experiences of being fed in this and other ways, children were being prompted to assemble, value, and learn to navigate these cultural models of relationships, shaping the social bonds that children were developing in culturally valued ways.

4.1 Food and Family in Viligama, Sri Lanka

Viligama is a twenty-minute bus ride from the provincial city of Kandy in the center of Sri Lanka. The people in this area are primarily Sinhala-speaking Theravada Buddhists, the numerically and politically dominant demographic on

---

[6] The ethnographic research and original analysis presented in this section was conducted by Bambi Chapin, one of the coauthors of this Element. This research was supported by the Fulbright Scholars Program and the National Institute of Mental Health, as well as university support. See Chapin (2014) for a fuller account of the material presented in this section.

the island. The families who have lived in Viligama a long time are mostly low- to middle-income, although the recently built housing scheme has drawn in new, sometimes more affluent families who do not socialize much with the longer-term residents of Viligama. Many in Viligama commute into the city for jobs and shopping and school, although there is also a free government school in the village, along with a Buddhist temple, a small clinic, and a post office. People work in construction, agriculture, manufacturing, civil service, banks, shops, and schools. Many have small enterprises of their own, driving a three-wheel taxi, making snacks, or offering tutoring. Some work abroad as house-maids, drivers, or accountants. Most families own their houses, usually with a little garden where they grow fruits, vegetables, and spices. Some have patty fields nearby to grow rice, the beloved daily staple. Everyone I knew, regardless of their primary occupations, grew at least a little of their own food and sometimes enough to sell.

4.1.1 Food and Eating

Food preparation is a major focus of most women's daily activities in Viligama, as well as a source of identity, interest, pride, and power. Most mothers I know, whether or not they work outside of the home, wake early to begin preparing the family's breakfast as well as lunch to send with those leaving for work or school. For Sinhala families, the ideal has long been for new couples to establish households of their own, leaving mothers responsible for housekeeping and caregiving. In practice, though, there are many kinds of households and family arrangements, with older parents living with grown children, relatives visiting for short and long periods, and the occasional person living alone.

On a typical day in many homes, the woman of the household may wake the others with "bed tea" or they may come to the kitchen for it. Breakfast might be a pancake-like savory *dosa* or boiled mung beans with coconut chutney, coconut *roti* with a chili and onion relish, or a bit of curry with rice, each person eating on their own schedule. Children are usually already washed and dressed for school by the time they are given breakfast. Later in the morning, there will usually be tea and a small snack, perhaps fried lentil balls (*vadee*) or commercially prepared biscuits. Lunch is traditionally the most substantial and significant meal of the day, usually consisting of a large plate of rice accompanied by a variety of spicy vegetable curries, as well as fish, egg, or occasionally chicken. Later in the day, there is typically another tea and snack, which may be more substantial for guests or for small children who may be sleepy by dinner time. Dinners, served shortly before the household heads to bed, are usually simpler than lunch, consisting of rice, noodles, or another starch served with curry or another accompaniment.

While mealtimes structure the days and are the focus of so much of women's work, family members do not typically eat together. On ordinary days in most households, each person eats as they are ready, with older people taking their plate to the dining area and eating with the fingertips of one hand and then washing their plate when they are finished. If it is a more celebratory meal, guests will be served and eat first, with men soon after. Women and any household helpers usually wait until their work is over and others have finished before taking a quiet moment to eat by themselves in the kitchen. Children eat whenever they seem ready, typically fed from a caregiver's hand.

Although meals are typically eaten without a display of enjoyment or praise for the cook, food is nonetheless the focus of a great deal of talk and pleasure. This is true of everyday meals as well as food at special celebrations or from the increasingly diverse range of restaurants in town. While each household cooks for itself, close relatives and neighbors will often send over portions of larger dishes, as well as extra uncooked vegetables or fruit. There are also occasions of shared eating that can be playful and intimate, with school friends or coworkers or even secret lovers sharing a single plate of food. Throughout these daily practices, food is used to instantiate and cement relationships.

4.1.2 Feeding Children

Feeding people is an important way that relationships are enacted in Sri Lanka, demonstrating a caring hierarchy and marking belonging. The act of feeding itself, particularly when it is done by hand, is emblematic of these relationships. One person placing food into another's mouth with their fingertips is part of ritual occasions as well as ordinary activities. It is the way that children are fed daily, from the time they start eating solid food throughout their school days and through adolescence (Figure 2).

Even before they begin eating solid food, children in Viligama and throughout the island are learning about the pleasures and dependability of being fed by caring and capable seniors. Babies are typically breastfed by their mothers, something that is not only expected but valued, often continuing for years, especially for youngest children. Children are nursed frequently and casually, which is something that both mothers and children are understood to enjoy. In the past, close female friends are said to have nursed each other's children, a practice that reverberates in the continued use of the affectionate term *kiri amma* (milk mother) to refer to an older woman with whom one has an especially close relationship. Children sleep next to their mothers, usually in a bed they share with their father and other young siblings. As children grow, they may move to a smaller bed in their parents' room, or to another room with a sibling or older relative, and

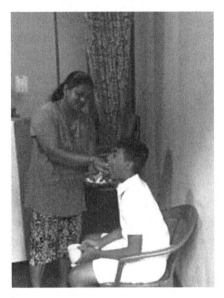

Figure 2 A Sinhala boy's visiting aunt feeds him breakfast before school.
© Bambi L. Chapin

eventually to their own room. It is not unusual for a child as old as eight or ten to still hold a mother's breast when the child is sleepy or wants comforting.

When I asked women about weaning, it was not usually something they had marked or even remembered as occurring at a particular age for a child. If mothers want their children to stop nursing, the usual method is to apply a bitter oil or other substance to the nipple without verbal explanations or negotiations with the child. Mothers remained responsive to children's initiation of nursing, conceptualizing it as something the child would decide whether to continue or not. This, as I will describe in Section 4.3, is in keeping with a model of hierarchical relationships in which seniors provide what they think their juniors need without explanation or negotiations, leaving juniors with the option to continue or not as they like.

It is the introduction of solid food rather than the cessation of breastfeeding that is marked as a developmental milestone by Sri Lankan parents. This first bite of solid food is ideally given at an auspicious time as part of a ceremony close to the child's sixth month. From that time forward, a child's mother or other (usually female) caregiver will make little balls of rice and curry from the plate she has dished up for the child and pop these balls into the child's open mouths. If there are several children of roughly the same age and ready to eat at the same time, they may be fed from the same plate. This manner of being fed continues for most children at meals at home throughout their growing up, even though they may eat by their own hand or utensils in other circumstances. Even when they become adults – perhaps returning home after a long time away, when they are sick, or in certain ceremonial occasions – mothers or other people in special relationships may feed them bites of food by hand in this same way.

4.2 An Ethnographic Encounter

By the middle of my first and longest research stay in Viligama in 2000–1, I had seen children being fed by hand many times. However, I had not really thought much about it until one morning when I was talking with my friend and neighbor, a woman I call Sii Devi.

On that particular morning, Sii Devi was complaining about her four-year-old niece who was staying with her. She said that the girl would not eat, that she would only eat milk and sweets, but she would not eat rice or fish. Thinking that my own four-year-old son would not eat fish either, I asked if her seven-year-old son liked fish. She said, "He eats it." Thinking that I had not been clear, I asked again if he *liked* it. Bemused, she said, "I don't know – he eats it." In response to my look of confusion, she said, "I feed it to him, so he eats it."

Suddenly, I saw these feeding episodes through new eyes. I began thinking about the assumptions that underlie them and were being communicated in them, the kinds of relationships that were being enacted and conveyed, the kind of choice-making that was or was not happening. As I went back through my notes and interview transcripts during that first period in the field, and as I paid new attention to these kinds of interactions and the ways that people talked about relationships between parents and children, I began to see the implicit cultural model of hierarchical relationships that Sinhala caregivers were drawing on and communicating to children in these interactions, models that children were assembling internally.

I also thought about the cultural models that shaped my own interactions with my son at mealtimes, taken-for-granted ways of interacting that my husband and I had brought with us from the United States. In the meals in our house, we sat together at a table, each feeding ourselves from our own plates, while Tucker's father and I coaxed him to "just give the fish a try," saying things like, "You can have the cucumbers or the green beans, but you have to have some vegetable," or "Take two more bites, and then you can have dessert," a pattern that is consistent with what Eli Ochs and her colleagues (1996) describe for other US families.

In each of these feeding patterns – both the one common in the United States where children are taught early to feed themselves and the one I saw in Sri Lanka where adults feed children by hand – children are ingesting more than food. They are physically experiencing valued relationship forms and the emotional orientations entailed in them. My son experienced something about himself as a choice maker and negotiator, with seniors who offer and limit options, with a premium on verbal expressiveness and physical separateness. The children I observed in Sri Lanka were learning that their seniors know what they need and will provide it and that the outcome will be satisfying and delicious. While the caregivers in these interactions – myself included – were just doing what seemed practical and usual in order to feed their children, the ways that this was done conveyed implicit notions about how people should interact.

4.3 A Cultural Model of Relationships

As I analyzed the data I had collected through observation, interviews, and casual conversation across a variety of topics and activities in Sri Lanka, a particular cultural model of ranked relationships emerged. In it, the person in the "good superior" role is expected to identify and provide what the junior person needs, without soliciting verbal input from the junior or justifying the actions. In this cultural model, good parents are sensitive to what their children need and respond to that knowledge without waiting for children to express the need directly or requiring them to verbalize it – what we call proactive caregiving in this Element. While doing this, parents and other senior people are expected to be kind and caring, confident and powerful, restrained and judicious.

For their part, the junior person should be compliant, passive, and respectful, without questioning or offering their own opinions. It is not, of course, that Sri Lankan children never demand things or assert their will. They do, and often quite insistently when they are very little, as I will discuss in Section 4.4. However, adults in Sri Lanka do not typically solicit these opinions or enter into extended negotiations around them of the type that Ochs and Kremer-Sadlik (2015) describe as common in middle-class family talk in the United States. Nonetheless, in feeding interactions as in other hierarchical relationships in Sri Lanka, the junior person's consent is required for the interaction to proceed. As they mature, young people in Sri Lanka are expected to demonstrate a growing capacity for self-control and good judgment, something they exercise as they choose what relationships to enter and whom to follow.

This model shows up and, I would argue, is conveyed to children not only in feeding but in all sorts of other daily interactions. It is evident in the ways, for instance, babies' urination and defecation are handled and how they learn to control it, something which is expected to have happened by the time a child is around nine months. Babies in Viligama typically wear little panties and are often laid on cloths which are changed as needed. A person who is holding a baby wearing such panties is highly attentive to subtle signs the child might be about to pee or poop and will swiftly hold them out away from their bodies. While adults do not do this to teach children a lesson, it is not surprising that a child who has the sensation of being whisked out into the air as soon as they begin to feel a need to urinate or defecate would learn to attend to their own bodily sensations and the need to act on them. As through feeding interactions, children are learning that their caregivers know what they need without the child needing to say anything and that the caregiver will respond to meet their needs as they see fit. As children grow, this relationship model continues to be enacted, reinforced, and complexified in their interactions with the parents and other senior people, something that is apparent in interactions at school, in marriage arrangements, at healthcare appointments, and during religious events.[7]

In addition to learning what to expect in hierarchical relationships, children are also learning what to expect from their peers through their everyday experiences. When multiple children in a household or family grouping are fed, it is sometimes from the same plate by the hand of a single caregiver. In these enactments, those sharing food experience both intimacy and sameness with these peers. They experience the idea and the ideal that those at the same position should have exactly the same and that close peers should share openly and without limits.

4.4 Responding to Children's Demands

This mode of interacting in which caregivers determine what children need and provide it, without waiting or encouraging the child to express their wishes, is not the only mode of interaction for Sri Lankan children and caregivers. I have regularly seen young children insisting on their own way, demanding what they want. They might be crying for their grandfather to go buy chocolate or their brother to hand over his ice cream or to sit on top of the dining table and ladle all of the coconut gravy onto their mother's plate.

This behavior did not stand out to me at first as particularly culturally shaped, I think because it was so in line with my own cultural expectations for toddler behavior and "the terrible twos," as we call them in the United States. What did surprise me and eventually captured my attention, though, was how their parents responded to them by eventually giving in to their demands, even if the demands seemed outrageous to me.

The seeds of this observation were present in the interaction with Sii Devi that morning. Although I had focused on the question of how she got her child to eat fish, she had originally been complaining that her niece would *not* – that she

---

[7] See Chapin (2014) for an account of this cultural model later in the life course and in other domains.

would only eat sweets. The implication was that, because of this, they were giving this girl only sweets. However, it was not until my second research visit to Sri Lanka a few years later, when I was actually staying in a home with a toddler, that I began to wonder why this indulgence did not seem to lead children to become demanding, "spoiled" older children and selfish adults.

What I came to observe was not just the material transaction in which demanding children got whatever they wanted if they screamed long enough but the emotional transaction. The mother of the child who is gleefully ladling all of the coconut curry is not stopping her, although she is clearly distressed about the waste. The boy who has to give his younger brother his ice cream is sulky and resentful. The grandfather who stopped by to see if his daughter needed anything on his way to the neighborhood shop feels bad that he has caused trouble. As I have argued at length elsewhere (Chapin, 2010), over time I believe that these children are learning to see that when they demand something, they might get it, but it will come with dislike, disapproval, and withdrawal.

All the while, these same children are having other experiences in which they say nothing and their caregivers provide what they need, as I have described in Section 4.3. Not only is the food tasty but the interaction is comforting, affectionate. They are accepted and cared for. As they grow, these children come to know that it is better to wait for what they are given. This good judgment is what people in Viligama referred to as "understanding" (*tereneva*), something that is thought to develop in children naturally, starting around five and certainly by ten. This social understanding prompts children to control themselves, to choose to follow the lead of worthy seniors, to enter into relationships with good people. These are the signs of maturity that people I knew in Sri Lanka expected of children as they grew, a kind of "intrapsychic autonomy" (see Ewing, 1991) marked by self-control rather than self-assertion (Chapin, 2013).

4.5 Variation and Social Change

While these patterns I have described are robust and widely recognizable to the people I work with in Sri Lanka, each instantiation is unique. They vary with circumstances and personal history, preference and resources. A woman who was responsible for feeding her younger brother and sister from the time she was eight years old while her mother worked abroad says she does not like to feed her own children by hand – and so she does not. The cheap packaged snacks and high-prestige fast food that children whine for are more available than they were twenty years ago and more affordable to many. Since these are not foods typically fed to children by hand, this shifts the balance and meaning of children's experiences that are mediated by food.

Further, both adults and children are agentive in these encounters. They draw on the cultural models they have to pursue a variety of goals. A teenage girl gives a special lunch packet to a boy she likes during a religious festival. Another girl refuses to eat with her friends to show them she is hurt. A teacher insists that a group of students who have been fighting share a lunch packet he gives them, suggesting they feed each other. Still angry, they refuse to go that far but agree to share it. Further, as children encounter new ways of interacting at schools with shifting pedagogical strategies and in interaction with an increasingly diverse media universe, these children bring new practices and possibilities for interacting back home with them and to the ways they will feed their own children in the future.

4.6 Conclusion

The ways that children are given food in Sri Lanka convey robust cultural models of relationships. As they physically experience the satisfaction and comfort of being fed by hand by caregivers who do not ask which bits they want next or what they think of the food, children are deriving lessons about what a good senior is – knowing, caring, and capable of meeting the needs of juniors – and about how they should behave with these seniors – deferent, patient, and acquiescent. As they are assembling these models of how the world and relationships work, they are drawing together similar experiences they have had – of breastfeeding, of learning to control their bladder, of going to bed. At the same time, they are drawing on contrasting experiences they have had – experiences of demanding what they thought they wanted, only to have it not turn out as they wished and with everyone annoyed with them. They come to realize that their parents really do know what is best for them.

5 Feeding and Food-Giving As a Proactive Caregiving System among the Tao in Taiwan

Between 2010 and 2011, I conducted twelve months of ethnographic fieldwork among the Indigenous Tao people on the Taiwanese island of Lanyu about the socialization and ontogeny of emotions (Funk, 2022; Funk et al., 2012; Röttger-Rössler et al., 2015).[8] I wanted to understand what kind of emotionally arousing socialization practices Tao caregivers apply to socialize and educate their children to become valuable individuals in their own society. Doing research

---

[8] The ethnographic research and original analysis presented in this section was conducted by Leberecht Funk, one of the coauthors of this Element. Research was funded by the German Research Foundation (DFG) and by the Cluster of Excellence "Language of Emotion" (2009–14) at the Free University of Berlin, Germany, which also provided a fifteen-month PhD scholarship (October 2015 to January 2017). Interviews were assisted by Xie Lai-Yu and Huang Ying-Zhen.

among the Tao was challenging for me since I was confronted with a cultural belief system that in many regards was opposed to my own German middle-class values. It took me several months to adapt to a local perspective on child-rearing, which at the same time meant that I had to deconstruct my own core beliefs through a self-reflective and sometimes painful process.

I propose that relationship formation among the Tao can only be fully under-stood if one considers the totality of the "developmental niche" (Super & Harkness, 1986) in which children grow up. The crucial importance of feeding and food-giving for human bonding emerges when one considers what is com-fortable and pleasant from a child's perspective. Being constantly exposed to an environment that is perceived as dangerous, it is mainly through feeding and food-giving that Tao children feel safe. I argue that there are two mutually related strands of emotion socialization that aim at protecting the "bodily self" (*kataotao*) in similar but different ways. The first strand of emotion socialization is related to ancestral taboo and is meant for teaching children how they can defend their bodily selves against the evildoings of malicious spirits. The second strand is related to proactive caregiving and oriented toward strengthening the bodily self primarily by nourishing it with food.

My insights are based on a mixed-method approach combining methods from social anthropology and developmental psychology. I spent uncountable hours in the village of Iranmeylek doing participant observation. A special feature of my research was that my former wife and our two sons, then aged eighteen months and five years, accompanied me during fieldwork. It is through them that I learned and understood many things about village life (Funk, 2020). With the help of two local field assistants, I conducted semi-structured interviews with caregivers about socialization practices, educational methods, cultural models of "person," "emotion," and "development," and childhood memories of elder Tao and children. My assistants and I also carried out a survey to determine the meaning of local emotion words. In addition, I systematically observed and documented emotional episodes between caregivers and children, as well as among peers (Röttger-Rössler, 2020).[9]

5.1 Food and Food Production in Tao Society

The Tao are one of the sixteen officially recognized Indigenous people of Taiwan. They number about 4,500 and live on the island of Lanyu, which is located 75 km off the southeastern coast of Taiwan. The interior of the island

---

[9] M. Holodynski, L. Funk, S. Jung, & B. Röttger-Rössler, *Coding Manual for Documenting Emotion Episodes*. Unpublished manual. Free University of Berlin, Cluster Languages of Emotion, 2010.

consists of volcanic mountain ranges covered with rainforest. There are six villages along a narrow coastal strip. The Tao had been living in relative isolation until the late 1960s when free access to the island began to be permitted by the Taiwanese government.

What Tao people do and say in their daily lives is often connected to the production, distribution, and consumption of food. The Tao's social organization, for example, can be analyzed in terms of food sharing: People are related to each other if they exchange food items and eat together on a regular basis (Funk, 2022; for examples from Southeast Asia, see Carsten, 1995, 1997 and Janowski & Kerlogue, 2007). Intergenerational relationships are characterized by a rigid age hierarchy, which is ultimately based on the fact that children are fed by older generations.

The most important meal is eaten in the late afternoon after all household members have returned from their activities. Traditional food (e.g., taro, sweet potato, fish, pork) is generally preferred over Chinese food (e.g., rice, noodles) but not always available. Among household members, food has to be shared but is not necessarily consumed together. Men and women eat together only if they belong to the same household, as commensality between unrelated individuals of the opposite sex has a sexual connotation and evokes intense feelings of mutual shame.

In the 1950s, many Tao converted to Catholicism and Presbyterianism. However, the belief in ancestral spirits has not ceased to exist. It is thanks to the ancestors that the Tao are able to feed themselves. The ancestors cultivated the land and planted the large trees needed for the construction of the large canoes that were used for catching flying fish before the introduction of motorboats in the 1980s. Up until today, each fish is treated with the utmost respect when it is cleaned, stored, and eaten. Ancestral insignia are hung at the fish drying racks to thank the ancestors for the catch. The Tao observe a large number of taboos, so that the holy swarm fish – the most important protein source available – is not offended and comes back to the shores of the island in plentiful quantities every year.

According to traditional views, the devastating typhoons that hit Lanyu in regular intervals are caused by the anger of the skygods who send these storms as revenge for human misconduct. In the past, typhoons were often followed by food shortages and occasionally even famines due to the salination of the taro fields (Yu & Dong, 1998). Until the 1960s, to eat to one's fill was nothing that could be taken for granted. Middle-aged and older Tao stressed how little they had to eat when they were children. Fighting over food in times of scarcity was also a topic repeatedly mentioned in the emotion stories.

Households and kinship groups display large quantities of food during important rituals and seasonal festivals. These so-called feasts of merit convey the social status of those who are able to produce greater quantities of food than others. According to tradition, newly built canoes and houses have to be fully covered with taro during inauguration ceremonies. At these occasions, pigs are sacrificed to the ancestors, and meat and tubers are distributed to those who helped during the construction process. People need to be involved in food exchange networks to maintain social relations with other households, otherwise they cease to be related to each other. The constant giving and taking of food ensures that all parties within a network enjoy maximum food security. However, kinship groups with only a few able-bodied workers do not manage to generate a major surplus, so they can only exchange food with a small number of partners. Not having many allies in the village, they have to endure the harassment of powerful others who steal their taro fields and other life resources (Funk, 2022; Yu, 1991).

5.2 Malicious Spirits, Fragile Souls, and Teasing

There is constant danger from malicious spirits who are called *anito* and delight in stealing human souls. Their favorite prey is young children who have not yet learned how to fix their souls to their bodily selves. In moments of fright, distress, or otherwise intense negative emotionality, young children's souls experience anxiety, which causes them to fly away in great panic. Without the soul properly attached to the body, a person soon becomes ill and – if no reunion takes place – eventually dies. To protect their children, Tao caregivers never leave them alone until approximately the age of three and a half years. Young children are always supposed to remain "calm" (*mahanang*) to assure that their fragile souls stay in place (Funk, 2014, 2022; Funk et al., 2012; Röttger-Rössler et al., 2015).

I have seen many times how toddlers were subjected to toughening up exercises that consistently follow the same pattern: Someone from a child's bilateral kinship group – often an elder cousin or sibling – sneaks up from behind and suddenly touches her beneath her shoulder. When she shrugs, relatives and unrelated villagers around her break out in great laughter – with the notable exception of her mother, who usually remains quiet. The only way for children to avoid these uncomfortable situations is to learn to suppress their startle responses and thus to actively anchor their souls to their bodies. This important developmental task is usually mastered around age three.

From late infancy onwards, Tao children are expected to regulate negative emotionality on their own. If they become angry, they are immediately scolded or shamed by laughing. Young children who cry for no socially acceptable reason (i.e., when they neither are in great pain nor suffer from soul loss) are scolded and threatened with a beating. Emotions such as anxiety, sadness, and anger are regarded as feeling states that overcome people in the context of spirit possessions. The *anito* inflict these emotions on children to misdirect their movements and speech acts because any weakening of their bodily selves makes it easier for them to snatch their souls.

Oftentimes, caregivers create scenarios similar to what Jean Briggs (1998) has termed "morality play": Young children are purposely drawn into situations from which they are at first not able to escape due to their immature physical and cognitive abilities. For instance, Tao caregivers hold crabs in front of infants' faces and laugh when they are afraid. Elders pinch toddlers while they are being held in their arms and show them their ulcers. Old women jokingly demand toys from young children. Old men throw angry looks at boys and pretend to beat them. Caregivers often irritate children to elicit angry reactions that are immediately shamed by laughing. Anxiety- and shame-inducing practices, which are considered great amusement, are usually continued until young children stay calm and avert their gaze. The culturally specific reason behind the systematic frightening, shaming, and teasing is to teach children to conceal socially disapproved emotions in their "deep insides" (*onowned*). Tao children learn that they cannot trust their own emotional impulses and that it is dangerous to allow oneself to be guided by one's immediate emotional responses (Funk, 2022).

5.3 Proactive Caregiving, Feeding, and Relatedness

It could be argued from the viewpoint of Western developmental psychology that the anxiety- and shame-inducing socialization practices that I have described so far evoke high degrees of psychological pressure on Tao children. They can only endure the uncomfortable teasing of their caregivers because there is a second strand of emotion socialization taking place at the same time, one which is centered around proactive caregiving and which is endowed with parental warmth and positive emotionality. It is especially through feeding that positive affective bonds are established between Tao children and their caregivers.

In infancy and early toddlerhood, Tao caregivers make use of proximal socialization strategies like primary care and body contact (Keller, 2007). Distal socialization strategies (e.g., face-to-face contact, baby talk), which feature prominently in Western psychological theories about "healthy" child development, are of minor importance. The Tao practice a form of multiple caretaking in which mothers, fathers, aunts, uncles, grandparents, and elder siblings are involved. Mothers view themselves as nourishers of their children. Their focus is on the fulfillment of children's physical needs. Today, mothers usually start giving formula milk after three to six months of breastfeeding. All mothers I talked to were convinced that powdered milk had better nourishing qualities than breastmilk. They gave it to their children so that their bodily selves would grow more quickly and become strong and healthy. When I asked mothers if they had experienced moments of "emotional intimacy" with their infants while breastfeeding, it was an alien concept for them with which none of them was familiar. In their view, what mattered most was that their children never stayed hungry and that sufficient food was provided.

In the Tao's language "to feel good" (*apiya so onowned*) primarily refers to a pleasant and comfortable bodily self and not so much to internal emotional states. Young children should always be able to eat what they want and as much as they want. Furthermore, children's body temperature should be neither too warm nor too cold, they should be washed every day, and their diapers should be changed immediately. Children whose needs are satisfied in these ways usually stay calm and are resistant to frustrations and other forms of distress. A pleasant body feeling helps them to keep their souls attached to their bodies.

Since the strict rules of the age hierarchy and the ban on crying do not allow children to appeal to caregivers in direct ways, their physical condition depends to a high degree on the empathic abilities of elder family members. Within the hierarchically organized kinship group, children cannot directly ask for food but have to wait until it is given to them. In many regards, the relationship between the Tao and their ancestors resembles the relationship between parents and children, as in both cases the latter depends on the former for the fulfillment of physical needs.

Tao children learn to evaluate social relationships by the amount and quality of food given to them. On one side of the spectrum, there are parents and other close relatives who provide them with the best food they can organize. On the other side, there are antagonistic kinship groups who view them as enemies and refuse to talk and share food with them. Most villagers take a position in between these extremes and give them some tidbits when there is plenty of food available, for example during festive activities. In these ways, from early on, the connections between kinship and food are emphasized. Tao kinship can be best described in terms of relatedness (Carsten, 2000) as it is social practice in the form of food-giving that brings people together as kin. This is also demonstrated by the fact that the Tao up until a few decades ago practiced milk kinship. If the mother had died or for some reason could not breastfeed her child, another lactating woman would give milk to the child instead. The life-saving gift was remembered by the village community, and the child was obliged to repay the wet nurse in her old age with food.

5.4 Growing Physical Autonomy and Changing Interactional Patterns

Most Tao children, due to the birth of younger siblings, experience intensive proactive caregiving for only a short period of time in their lives. In Tao society, physical autonomy is highly valued and physical dependency on caregivers is not artificially prolonged. Eighteen-month-olds are not spoon-fed anymore but usually eat on their own. However, they are socially excluded if they do not know how to behave themselves during family meals. The reason behind this exclusion is of a spiritual nature: If children (or adults) get angry during meals, or otherwise produce loud noise, all of the food has to be discarded. The strict rules for eating teach children in early toddlerhood that food is a serious matter, nothing they can play with but rather something that is only provided under the condition that they respect the ancestral laws.

From two years onward, caregivers increasingly make use of verbal instructions that highlight the negative consequences of incorrect behavior. If toddlers do not listen to their caregivers and hurt themselves, they will be laughed at. They are only comforted once they have stopped crying. In this way, children learn that they are responsible for their bodily selves and that they can only ward off evil harm if they listen to the words of respected elders.

From two and a half years onward, caregivers refuse to hold children in their arms or to carry them around. For many children, the sudden lack of body contact is hard to bear. Longing for physical contact, children between three and nine years repeatedly asked me to hug them. For the same reason, I saw them approaching Taiwanese tourists.

By age three and a half, children are expected to put on their clothes by themselves and take care of their own personal hygiene. This is also the age when they start running away when their caregivers threaten to beat them for being naughty. The growing physical autonomy drives Tao children into the arms of their peers with whom they will spend the bulk of their time from then on roaming about the village and its adjacent areas. They only return home if they are hungry or tired. Adults usually do not get involved in children's affairs. Much of the emotional intimacy that, from a Euro-American middle-class perspective, is expected to be inherent in caregiver–child relationships can be found in relationships among age-mates. The local word for "same-aged friend" (*kagagan*) literally means "the one with whom one laughs together."

5.5 Sweet Potatoes Instead of Teddy Bears

A prototypical episode that occurred several times in the emotion stories people told and that I repeatedly observed myself starts with a child around the age of three

(a)   (b)

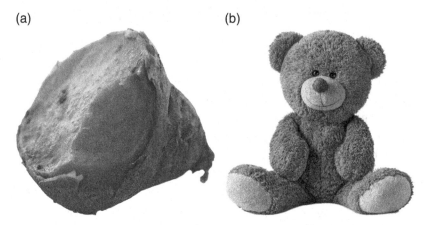

Figure 3 Two culturally specific replacements of the mother: (a) a piece of sweet potato (Tao people) and (b) a teddy bear (Euro-American middle classes). © iStock

having been left behind by his mother who has gone to the fields. The mother sneaks away clandestinely, as she can neither take him with her (the *anito* would snatch his soul) nor tell him where she is going (his soul would follow her). The child either wakes up and cannot find his mother or he tries to follow her but cannot keep up with her. In both cases, the child cries and/or throws tantrums, sometimes pulling his hair. His aunts and grandmothers, who always watch over him, "comfort him with food" (*ipowring*) – sweet potatoes until the 1980s, today usually sweets – which has an immediate calming effect on him. When children are upset, they are generally often pacified by their caregivers through food-giving.

The food young Tao children hold in their hands in moments of distress is comparable to a puppet or teddy bear in a Western context: In both cultural traditions, an imaginary part of the mother remains with the children and helps them to stay calm and feel secure (Figure 3). For Tao children, the replacement of the mother does not need to have a face with eyes and a mouth because what counts in this sociocultural setting is not *psychic-emotional intimacy* but *physical material warmth* in the shape of food. This, however, does not mean that physical-material warmth does not have an emotional component; rather, the emotions involved in physical material warmth are predominantly expressed through the exchange of food or by acting in supporting ways, but not so much through shared mental worlds.

5.6 Feeding, Food-Giving, and Ancestral Knowledge As a Form of Self-Help

The physical security Tao children enjoyed during infancy and early toddlerhood due to the proactive caregiving style of their caregivers is severely threatened around the age of three and a half when children increasingly have to care for themselves as autonomous agents. From the viewpoint of Western psychology, the seemingly harsh socialization practices and the reduction of caregiving measures lead to a crisis in early childhood that is experienced by Tao children as a time of deprivation. The only warmth they still receive is produced by the ongoing intergenerational feeding relationship, which continues into the onset of adulthood. From early toddlerhood onward, intergenerational feeding relationships are transformed into physically more distant relationships that are characterized by the giving and receiving of food. All further processes of relationship formation are channeled into this culturally specific developmental pathway.

However, children are grateful not only when elders provide food for them but also when parents teach them traditional skills and abilities. The ancestral knowledge passed down from father to son and from mother to daughter serves as instruction for self-help, as a guidance for physical survival in a sometimes difficult and dangerous environment. It consists, among other things, in instructions about how to produce food, for example where and when it is best to catch octopus, or how to dig out ceremonial taro. The transmission of knowledge, which carries the words of the ancestors, is the ultimate stage of physical distancing in which parents begin to transform into ancestral beings. Since ancestral knowledge is not freely shared with everyone, it has to be perceived as a blessing that is only passed on to those who listen to their parents and observe the ancestral taboos.

Before the introduction of whole-day schooling in the early 1980s, young Tao could still overcome their anxiety and shame disposition by intruding bravely into areas haunted by malicious spirits (e.g., taro fields, mountain forests, the deep sea) for reasons of food production. As food providers for others, they enjoyed a higher social status, which made them feel proud in their insides. This traditional developmental pathway is now widely blocked as young individuals lack time and opportunity to engage in subsistence activities.

5.7 Conclusion

Feeding and food-giving are the determining factors for human bonding in Tao society because the provision with food is of paramount importance for physical as well as psychological survival. To have food at one's disposal does not simply mean that there is enough to eat; it indicates that ancestral bonds are undisturbed and that one is being cared for and not alone. In addition, it defines one's social status and signifies that one behaves in a morally correct manner. The giving of food produces a "feeling of calmness" (*mahanang so onowned*) within the Tao that arguably bears similarities with the Western notion of a "feeling of security," one of the key concepts used in attachment theory (Funk, 2022).

Throughout life, children and adults remain dependent on the blessings of their ancestors. Only if the Tao follow the ancestral laws will their bodily selves be protected from evil harm and will they be able to produce enough food to live an affluent life. The emotions involved in the intergenerational feeding relationship are anxiety and respect but also a deep-rooted thankfulness toward elder generations and ancestors.

Emotion socialization and relationship formation among the Tao can only be understood if one takes a holistic perspective. Proactive caregiving, especially feeding and food-giving, and the constant frightening, shaming, and teasing of young children by their caregivers ultimately serve the same aim: They ensure that children stay always in a calm state in which their fragile souls are firmly attached to their bodily selves.

6 Attachment Formation through Breastfeeding and Feeding: Insights from Urban Middle-Class Families in San José, Costa Rica

In this ethnographic section, I investigate the meaning of feeding for the formation of attachment in highly educated middle-class families in urban Costa Rica. During my twenty-three-month research stay from 2019 to 2021, I participated in a study of the development of attachment in different cultural groups residing in Costa Rica.[10] The study with San José middle-class families is part of this study program. San José is the capital of Costa Rica, with a concentration of academic, political, economic, and cultural centers offering a wide range of occupational fields with many middle-class jobs (Rosabal-Coto, 2012). There is a wide range of health services, both public and private, for prenatal, childbirth, and postpartum care. Our findings revealed that the feeding network, namely who participates in feeding the child, seems to regulate the attachment network. Also, feeding practices function as socialization mechanisms that promote both children's autonomy and their connectedness to the family.

6.1 Children's Socialization in San José

Previous research has shown that San José middle-class families share dimensions with both rural non-Western populations and what Henrich et al. (2010) dubbed "WEIRD" populations – Western, Educated, Industrialized, Rich, and

---

[10] The ethnographic research and original analysis presented in this section was conducted by Wiebke J. Schmidt, one of the coauthors of this Element. The data were collected as part of the research project "Cultural Conceptions of Attachment in Costa Rica," led by Prof. Dr. Mariano Rosabal-Coto and Prof. em. Dr. Heidi Keller. The research was funded by the Sievert Foundation for Science and Culture, a grant award of the Costa Rica Zentrum of Osnabrück University, Germany, and the University of Costa Rica, Costa Rica.

Democratic. For example, parental ethnotheories among these families are oriented toward traditional cultural values like *familismo* (i.e., family loyalty, closeness, and placing importance on family needs over individual needs [Sotomayor-Peterson et al., 2012]). Extended family members often live nearby and are highly involved in childcare, especially grandparents who are often addressed as *Mamá* and *Papá*. Good demeanor and orientation toward the family are important socialization goals (Rosabal-Coto, 2012). Accordingly, children are expected to show respect in everyday interactions. Even children as young as three are expected to greet visitors appropriately when they enter the house.

At the same time, however, childcare and family life have been undergoing transformations in recent decades with many middle-class families in San José now sharing characteristics with typical WEIRD families, such as high formal education and nuclear households with few children and displaying values associated with the US middle class (De Jeude et al., 2016). Parental ethnotheories are also starting to change, including adopting the belief that the mother is the natural primary caregiver, that children should always be at the center of attention, and that parenting includes high material and emotional investments (Fallas Gamboa & Solís Guillén, 2020). While the proximal parenting style, characterized by body contact and body stimulation (Keller, 2007), is traditionally common in Costa Rica and still prevalent in rural areas (Rosabal-Coto, 2012), San José middle-class families increasingly show the distal parenting style, characterized by face-to-face interactions with the involvement of an object often in the form of a toy, accompanied by much verbalization. In interactions, caregivers tend to follow the child's lead in a responsive manner. Dyadic caregiver–child play with a strong emphasis on positive emotionality is common and seen as an opportunity to educate and stimulate the child (Schmidt et al., 2021, 2023a). At the same time, the awareness among caregivers of attachment theory is increasing due to the promotion in public services. For example, in our interviews with childcare experts and in the publicly available information material provided by the Ministry of Health (Ministerio de Salud, 2012), the formation of a secure attachment was considered as one of the most important developmental goals in the early years and elemental to the formation of trust, security, and the ability to have healthy and fulfilling relationships in adulthood. Therefore, many parents in the study felt that the development of trust and security was one of the most important socialization goals for their children.

6.2 The Meaning of Food

Food plays a special role in San José family life, and extended family members are often involved in feeding children (Sedó Masís & Ureña Vargas, 2007), similarly to what has been reported for rural Moroccan families in the first ethnographic section. A healthy diet is considered fundamental for children's development. While it is common in rural regions of Costa Rica for families to grow some of their own food (or even most of it in Indigenous communities), in San José it is bought in supermarkets and at farmers' markets. Rice and beans, often served with meat or fish, vegetables, and plantains, are the basic foods that are an integral part of breakfast, lunch, and dinner. Although baby food is available in supermarkets, children are usually accustomed to the local food from six months of age. However, increased availability of nonlocal food items (i.e., "fast food," processed foods) has influenced dietary choices, including mothers' and children's diets (Cantor et al., 2013). In general, the constant availability and accessibility of food is taken for granted in the urban middle class, whereas food insecurity still exists in poorer families in urban and especially rural regions of the country.

6.3 The Present Study

The local research team and I conducted interviews with a total of sixty-nine caregivers of thirty families with a child between six and nineteen months. These interviews always included the mother and sometimes also included fathers, grandparents, uncles, or aunts. Parents in this sample are highly educated, waiting for their first child until they could count on economic stability and were living together with their spouse (at approximately age thirty) and forming a nuclear family with one or two children. Although I identify as a "young, white German woman," the participants and I shared that we were college-educated, mostly with university degrees, and middle class. Most members of the local research team were also middle class and almost all were from the San José region. We visited the families at home, often several times, interviewing everyone who participated in childcare. During the analysis, the interview codes focused on the feeding network, feeding practices, including breastfeeding, links between feeding and attachment formation, emotions and experienced difficulties associated with feeding, and traditions and socialization goals associated with feeding. In addition, the team took photographs of the environment and video recordings of everyday interactions between children and caregivers.

Additionally, the team interviewed six childcare experts based in San José (e.g., pediatrician, midwife, representative of La Leche League). According to the childcare experts, parents often seek professional help for breastfeeding and feeding issues. Also, in San José, parenting programs and guidelines that the experts use and refer to are often derived from attachment theory. Accordingly, childcare professionals sensitize families about the importance of the attachment relationship between child and caregiver, mostly the mother.

6.4 Breastfeeding As an Important Attachment Mechanism

Sixteen out of the thirty participating families reported the mother being the person primarily responsible for feeding the infant. In these sixteen families, the mother was breastfeeding the infant. The remaining fourteen families reported shared feeding responsibilities among caregivers. Seven of these families had never breastfed exclusively and reported shared feeding responsibilities since the infant's birth. In total, only four children in the sample were fed exclusively by the mother at the time of the interview. In contrast, the vast majority of children were regularly fed by several caregivers, something that increased with the age of the child. Multiple caregivers, including having multiple people providing feeding, is a feature shared by families living in the majority world and also by many families from Western contexts where paid childcare and fathers' involvement are common (Keller & Chaudhary, 2017).

While caregivers in the study associated exclusive breastfeeding with the belief that feeding fosters attachment (*apego*, understood as an affective, profound relationship that is consistent during most of a person's life, mostly with parents and other close family members), early bottle-feeding was associated with the belief that feeding is primarily alimentary without attachment-related functions. Interestingly, families in which the child was breastfed reported that feeding in general, not only breastfeeding, fostered attachment. Accordingly, the ability to breastfeed exclusively turned out to be a key factor in specifying whether caregivers considered feeding to be relevant for attachment formation. One breastfeeding mother explained, "I believe that breastfeeding was the number one source of nourishment and that the bond that I had with him in the early months through breastfeeding is something that no one else can give him – it's a sacred time." Another mother reported that she believes that breastfeeding fulfills non-alimentary functions: "Breastfeeding is extremely important, mainly because of the affection the children have with you, and they feel more secure when you breastfeed them, and I feel that their way of learning is also different, not that they wouldn't have the same capabilities, but, I don't know, they adapt faster to certain activities when you breastfeed them." Childcare experts confirmed that many breastfeeding mothers believe they have a unique relationship with their infants through breastfeeding. Mothers are proud of this close relationship and enjoy the intimate dyadic setting.

6.5 Responsive Caregiving and Feeding

Infants were expected to communicate to caregivers when they are hungry, and caregivers were expected to always and promptly respond to these signals, consistent with the concept of responsive feeding (WHO, 2009). Caregivers usually responded to these signals by first asking the child what he or she wanted or needed. This pattern reflects the status of children as quasi-equal partners from early on who have the lead in interactions. Young, especially breastfed, children usually directed the request for food primarily to the mother. The breastfeeding situation was an intimate, dyadic moment between mother and child, characterized by face-to-face contact and the exchange of positive emotions and expressions (including baby talk). The mother usually retreated to a quiet place for breastfeeding, sat down comfortably, and concentrated entirely on the baby (Figure 4).

The participant mothers reported wanting to breastfeed for approximately two years. However, many emphasized they would continue breastfeeding as long as their child wanted to, reflecting the prioritization of the child's will. In line with this, weaning was understood as an important detachment process between mother and child for which both must feel ready. "Baby-led weaning" was a popular approach among San José middle-class families, introducing

Figure 4 Intimate moment between mother and infant during breastfeeding. © Wiebke J. Schmidt

There is eye contact between mother and child, the mother smiles and speaks gently to her son, praising him for eating well while lovingly playing with his hand. Breastfeeding usually takes place in an exclusive and dyadic setting.

solids at six months so that, instead of pureed food, babies were given chunks of solid food. Through self-feeding, children controlled their intake of food. At the same time, it served as a playful exploration of food and the development of food preferences (Gomez et al., 2020). Children were usually placed in a seat and presented with various finger foods prepared for them (e.g., peeled, cut into pieces). They were encouraged to try the food they are given and praised extensively if they did, with caregivers mirroring the child's reactions to different foods with facial expressions and verbalizations ("Oh, you didn't like that at all, yuck!" or "Hmm yummy, you want more of that!"). Increasingly, more caregivers (e.g., grandmothers, aunts) are involved in feeding and preparing food for the child, and this difference is most noticeable among previously breastfed children. For caregivers as well as children, feeding was usually a cheerful activity enjoyed by everybody. With increasing age, children were expected to adapt to family meals, eating with the family at the table and eating what is served. However, negotiating over food and expressing one's own likes and dislikes remained common. Parents generally see themselves as role models of healthy eating for their older children, so they want to model for them eating enough fruits and vegetables, at regular times, and not too much fast food (Núñez Rivas et al., 2013).

6.6 The Feeding Network Regulates the Attachment Network

For bottle-fed and breastfed infants, similar caregiver networks and arrangements were reported. However, families in which the mother breastfed exclusively mostly reported exclusive maternal attachment, while those families in which the child was bottle-fed from early on reported multiple attachments to those persons involved in feeding the child. Thus, children in this sample seem to be attached to those people who feed them, which contradicts Bowlby's (1958, 1969) view that feeding plays only a marginal, if any, role in the development of attachment. Further, the caregivers clearly stated that it is the feeding itself – not only the body contact or warmth that goes along with it – that fosters attachment formation. This becomes especially clear when caregivers explain why the breastfeeding mother is the child's favorite person, like this mother: "Obviously I am like everything she needs in terms of food at the moment, so that bond that we have is unique, and obviously she will prefer me." Some parents even reported differences between the attachments of children in the same family based on their feeding practices. As one mother described, "I didn't breastfeed Sebastian that much, I breastfed him for about four months, and Mateo until he was a year old, and I feel that, I don't know, that's why his [Mateo's] bond is very close with me." Her husband agreed, adding, "My wife always breastfeeds Mateo to make him fall asleep, while I always used to put Sebastian to sleep by feeding him with the bottle, that's why Sebastian is more attached to me."

Bottle-feeding families named those persons who regularly fed their child as having a closer relationship with the child, yet they did not specify the reason, as breastfeeding mothers did. The childcare experts explained that families who unsuccessfully attempted to breastfeed suffer from strong feelings of frustration and guilt, which sometimes lead to a kind of defense or coping mechanism in which the attachment-related functions of feeding are not considered. This is reflected in a mother's description of how she reacted when she realized she was not able to breastfeed: "I got so frustrated, I got very frustrated because I felt that I was not doing my best, for me as a mom this pregnancy and this child was specifically complicated because of my expectations, maybe not because of the reality but the expectations of what I wanted, of what I expected." This further illustrates that feeding is a very emotional topic associated with social pressure, highly dependent on "success" in breastfeeding or other feeding techniques (e.g., baby-led weaning). Caregivers feel joy and pride when they feel that they successfully master it – and shame and guilt when they feel their children are not eating as expected.

6.7 Eating and Sharing Food As a Social Activity

Socialization goals and traditions are evident in everyday mealtime situations in San José middle-class families. Children are expected to learn that mealtimes are a social activity shared with the family. Typically, the entire household shares at least one meal a day together, depending on working hours and other arrangements. Mothers and grandmothers often do the cooking and serve the food to the rest of the family members, who sit around a table in the living room. Already, toddlers are taught to show good manners, such as not to play when eating and sitting nicely on the chair, and older children are involved in making traditional food for special occasions (e.g., *tamales* for Christmas). Many caregivers reported regular family dinners with extended family members to be an important social activity in their daily life, with a cheerful atmosphere, family interaction, and children being involved from early on. Thus, mealtimes represent a common setting to teach traditions and cultural values like respect, reflecting the preservation of traditional *familismo* values in an otherwise much individualized world (De Jeude et al., 2016). Interestingly, food seems to promote the development of autonomy at the same time, especially with increasing age; children are expected to have and express their own food preferences, let caregivers know when and what they want to eat, and learn to eat independently. The fact that sharing food also serves as an expression of connection and affection in adolescence and adulthood becomes especially clear when visiting relatives. Grandmothers and other women of the older generation are always expected to offer large amounts of delicious food when the younger generations come to visit (often without notice). When the younger people leave, the hosts often insist that leftovers from the meal be packed and taken away, often to bring it to other family members.

6.8 The Influence of Expert Knowledge

The Costa Rican Health Ministry strongly recommends exclusive breastfeeding for the first six months (following WHO guidelines; WHO, 2009). To promote breastfeeding, they published a national policy for breastfeeding (Ministerio de Salud, 2009) and a *Manual for the Implementation of Breastfeeding Clinics in Hospital Settings* (Ministerio de Salud, 2012). They also offer educational material for caregivers that recommends breastfeeding based on health-related arguments but also on expected benefits for the mother–child attachment relationship (Ministerio de Salud, 2012).

Both caregivers and childcare experts agreed that families invest many resources (time, money) in seeking advice from experts in the form of classes, books, and counseling on feeding issues. Intergenerational knowledge transfer is still common; however, most parents trust more in professional knowledge. The variety of advice was overwhelming sometimes, and many parents reported feeling high societal pressure to feed their children in the correct way. One family described how they went to see three different experts because the mother did not seem to produce sufficient milk, and they still felt criticized by friends for not trying hard enough to breastfeed. Motherhood in general and breastfeeding as a part of it are often idealized before birth, so that reality and unexpected difficulties hit hard. The parental stress induced by high expect-ations regarding breastfeeding, especially for mothers who are not able to breastfeed, represents the "other side" of pushing for natural feeding solutions.

6.9 Conclusion

This study demonstrated that caregivers in the San José middle class perceive feeding, and especially breastfeeding, as an important attachment mechanism. However, the belief that feeding is relevant for attachment formation is highly dependent on the feeding practices the caregivers use, such as whether the mother breastfeeds her child or not. Feeding is not understood as mere food intake; it can represent an intimate moment filled with positive emotions between caregiver and child. Moreover, feeding and eating are a fundamental part of children's socializa-tion in San José, promoting the development of both autonomy and relatedness and the formation of egalitarian relationships between caregivers and children.

7 Comparison of Results and Theoretical Analysis

As unique as each of the communities presented in this Element are, together they have important things to show us about the role of feeding in shaping social and emotional bonds between children and the world of people – and sometimes spirits – in which they are growing up. In this section, we discuss the theoretical implications of the feeding practices presented in the previous ethnographic sections. First, we compare the feeding practices in our research sites and, on this basis, challenge the globally applied norms of feeding that we have outlined in the introduction. Second, we analyze the consequences of these feeding practices for relationship formation and discuss them with regards to attachment theory, arguing for a new theoretical framework that allows the inclusion of multiple forms of attachment. In doing so, we highlight the distinction between physical and psychological aspects of care, as well as the enduring social, emotional, and spiritual connections with important others that are largely ignored in the dominant literature. We advocate for a shift away from supposedly universal norms to an effort to understanding development as it unfolds in diverse sociocultural contexts. When referring to our field sites, we use country names as a matter of convenience. However, these should always be read as place markers for the specific locales and groups that were studied by our team members.

7.1 Norms and Variations in Feeding

Across our case studies, as well as in the pediatric literature in which universal feeding norms are proclaimed (Black & Aboud, 2011; Pérez Escamilla et al., 2021), at least three dimensions of feeding practices emerge: food and eating arrangements; feeding through the life course; and different modes of inter-action that can be analytically framed by the concepts of responsive and proactive feeding. In the following, we discuss these three dimensions to highlight the implications of our research for the mainstream science of feeding.

7.1.1 Food and Eating Arrangements

Food and eating arrangements across the five ethnographic settings differ from each other in significant ways, as we describe briefly in what follows. There are few common patterns of what people eat, how they categorize foods, or how meals are socially and temporally arranged. This indicates that if we are to understand the role of intergenerational feeding for human bonding, we must examine these practices in specific circumstances right from the beginning.

The most important staple foods differ across our field sites: bread in Morocco, rice in Madagascar and Sri Lanka, rice and beans in Costa Rica, and taro and fish in Taiwan. In Sri Lanka, Morocco, and Costa Rica, a large variety of foods and spices is used. Families in Madagascar, by contrast, focus on a few foods only and traditionally use just salt as a seasoning. Here, limited food diversity is part of a value system in which only a small number of foods are considered to be healthy and nourishing (e.g., rice, beef) while others are considered to be inferior. In Madagascar, as well as in Taiwan, food choices are limited by taboo.

In all settings, we find different food categories. In the Taiwanese and Malagasy settings, for example, people differentiate between "ritual foods" and "mundane foods." Meat is traditionally only eaten after pigs (Taiwan) and cattle (Madagascar) have been sacrificed to the ancestors. When eating "ritual foods," certain rules and taboos must be observed. A special feature of Tao eating culture is the classification of fish into men's and women's fish, which have to be eaten from different plates. Furthermore, in all settings there is a differentiation between regular "meals" and irregular "snacks" (e.g., candies, potato chips, wild fruits), with children eating the latter outside of the context of family meals. In many cases, different meanings and practices are associated with snacks as compared to meals, which we describe in our ethnographic cases.

In the ways in which regular meals are arranged, we find some commonalities as well as differences. In each setting, it is mostly mothers or other female relatives who prepare meals, which are then consumed by family members. The timing of these meals varies considerably, with Moroccan families eating four meals a day and people in Madagascar eating only two. In some contexts, meals follow a relatively fixed schedule as in Costa Rica, Morocco, and Sri Lanka; while in Madagascar and Taiwan, their timing varies greatly.

The size and composition of groups who regularly eat together also differ considerably. While in Morocco and Costa Rica, household members regularly eat together with extended kin, this is not the norm in the other settings where family members eat separated by gender or sequentially. Eating in small, gendered groups is most pronounced in Madagascar, where people withdraw temporarily for eating even during festivities. While families in Taiwan, Madagascar, and Morocco typically eat from common plates or bowls, people in Costa Rica and Sri Lanka usually eat from their own plates. In Costa Rica and Morocco, food is usually consumed while sitting around a table, whether on chairs or cushions. In Sri Lanka, people often eat just sitting on a chair. In Madagascar and Taiwan, people traditionally eat while sitting on the floor without tables. Further, the order of eating and the ideas associated with it differ across our settings: While families in Costa Rica and Morocco emphasize the importance of conviviality, people in Madagascar and Taiwan insist on sequential beginnings and endings of eating according to age hierarchy, gender, and rank. In Sri Lanka, an order related to age and gender is preferred but flexible in practice.

7.1.2 Feeding and Eating through the Life Course

In the course of a person's life, feeding and eating practices change, particularly in the first years of life. Pediatrics and nutritional scientists have established standards for transitions in feeding practices that are considered optimal for child development and are globally promoted through UN agencies and other organizations (e.g., WHO, 2009). According to these standards, children should be breastfed exclusively for the first six months, after which mother's milk should be complemented by porridge and finger foods. In the second year, children should begin to eat independently and participate in regular family meals. Our studies show that life course changes in feeding practices vary greatly between the studied groups and, in many cases, diverge from these allegedly optimal standards.

In each of the communities we profile, children are (or used to be) breastfed for their first two years. Formula is used to replace mother's milk in some settings but not in Madagascar or Sri Lanka. In several cases, mothers breast-feed their last children considerably longer, for instance up to the age of seven in Madagascar, which points to the fact that the birth of younger siblings strongly influences the duration of breastfeeding. Solid foods are introduced in addition to breastfeeding and formula in each of our settings between four and six months, which is more or less in line with international feeding guidelines.

In each of the settings other than Sri Lanka, caregivers encourage children to self-feed from an early age, usually around one or two. In the Sri Lankan case, however, caregivers commonly hand-feed their children until adolescence and, at occasions, into adulthood. Obviously, caregivers do not continue this practice because children are unable to feed themselves. Rather, it is continued because hand-feeding establishes a way to build and maintain close and affectionate hierarchical relationships within the family. According to the standards of responsive feeding, however, prolonged feeding is believed to interfere with children's autonomy development, pathologizing such culturally valued feeding practices.

This diversity of feeding practices we have documented calls into question the universality of the type of feeding declared and enforced by developmental theories, something we return to in Section 8.3.

7.1.3 Modes of Interaction: Responsive and Proactive Feeding

Finally, we discuss the role allocations between caregivers and children within feeding interactions with a particular focus on the aspect of control. Advocates of responsive feeding proclaim that caregivers should feed their children in response to their expressions of hunger and satiety. In the responsive feeding interaction, children are assumed to know best what and how much to eat and are encouraged to assume an active role by expressing their wants and wishes. The caregivers assume an assisting, passive role that becomes dispensable as soon as children are able to self-feed.

By contrast, in what we are calling the proactive feeding interaction, the role allocations between children and caregivers are reversed: Here it is not the children but the caregivers who are believed to know best what kind of food and how much of it is good for children to eat. The active role of caregivers may be maintained even after children have become capable of self-feeding. Children assume a receiving role and may learn to trust in their caregiver's decisions and to appreciate their care.

It is important to note that both responsive and proactive feeding styles are ideal types. Neither interactional style can exist in a pure form as there are always shades in between. A proactive feeding style does not mean that caregivers ignore the signals sent by children; nor does a responsive feeding style imply that children are allowed to do whatever they want. Rather than being arranged as a dichotomy, the two feeding styles can be viewed as end poles of a spectrum, with some practices falling in the middle.

Among our cases, only caregivers in Costa Rica emphasized the importance of following children's lead when feeding, which also includes the idea of baby-led weaning. When solid foods are introduced, they are typically given choices of finger foods that enable them to practice self-feeding and to develop personal preferences from an early age onward. This is in line with the ideology of responsive feeding, according to which children know instinctively how much and what kind of food they need and prefer. As in Costa Rica, Moroccan children actively articulate food preferences during family meals, to which mothers usually respond. However, Moroccan caregivers do not exclusively attend to children's wishes as the overall focus is on commensality and conviviality with the extended family. Children learn that they are not always the focus of attention and occasionally have to wait until food is passed on to them. Therefore, feeding in Morocco could be described as neither primarily responsive nor proactive but as something in between.

In other settings, feeding practices are clearly proactive. In Sri Lanka, caregivers know what food is good for children and when they need to eat, placing each bite into children's open mouths. While children express hunger and satiation, Sri Lankan mothers do not typically ask children to select foods or to express opinions about what and how much they eat; nor do they insist that children feed themselves. In Madagascar, mothers frequently offer their breasts to children without any obvious signals from their offspring. While these mothers may still respond to subtle bodily cues from their babies, their feeding practice mostly preempts explicit expressions of hunger or desire for particular foods. In older children and adults, such expressions are frowned upon. The situation in Taiwan today has changed in that caregivers try to fulfill children's food preferences but nevertheless expect them to remain quiet and to wait until food is served to them.

As with the types and arrangements of eating in these communities, the understandings, emotional tones, and valued behaviors in these interactions between caregivers and children not only vary across these groups but do so in many ways that are at odds with expectations for ideal child feeding set out by developmental experts.

7.2 Feeding and Relationship Formation

While in all settings feeding contributes to relationship formation, it does so in different ways. Our material points to three different socio-emotional dimensions of feeding, each of which plays a role in the development of relationships: First, the *proximal dimension*, which refers to the physical feeding interaction; second, the *transactional dimension*, referring to the fact that food is given and received; third, the *distal dimension*, meaning that feeding can be an occasion for co-occurring interaction and sociality. Usually, all dimensions are present in feeding. Breastfeeding, for example, is proximal in that caregivers offer their breasts while children are drinking, it is transactional since caregivers give milk and children take it, and it is distal since breastfeeding is an occasion for additional interactions like eye contact or verbal interactions. Even though these dimensions are co-occurring in all five settings, they are emphasized and elaborated in different ways.

7.2.1 Feeding As a Physical Interaction (Proximal Dimension)

In infancy, the proximal dimension is important in all settings, simply because young children cannot feed themselves. However, this dimension of feeding is particularly emphasized in Sri Lanka, where caregivers continue to hand-feed children throughout childhood and, under some conditions, beyond. That children as old as eight may still hold their mother's breast for comfort points to the significance of feeding for attachments in Sri Lanka. Here, parents and others express their caring affection through hand-feeding, and children in turn experience hand-feeding as comforting and enjoyable. It allows them also to learn to trust that their caregivers know and do what is good for them.

Continued hand-feeding is part of a model of hierarchical relationships that is also enacted and communicated through other caregiving practices.[11] Sri Lankan

---

[11] The use of food and feeding as a way to enact physical closeness in childhood and beyond is emphasized in other societies as well (see, for instance, spoon-feeding in Vietnam [Scheidecker et al., 2021] and among Chinese immigrants in the United States [Zhou et al., 2015]).

children experience a clear role division between food provider and receiver, which is expressed on a physically intimate level. It is important to note, however, that children are not forced to comply with their caregivers' feeding but rather are understood to do so voluntarily. If children voice demands, caregivers will usually fulfill their wishes but rather reluctantly, putting the intergenerational harmony under stress. Thus, positive mutual feelings are experienced when children actively agree to accept the treatments of elders. The crucial point is that children choose to trust in their caregivers and that children therefore must be viewed as persons endowed with agency. Therefore, autonomy and relatedness are intertwined in almost inseparable ways. Importantly, proximal feeding also occurs in egalitarian relationships in Sri Lanka, with peers, secret lovers, and spouses engaging in mutual hand-feeding or eating by hand from the same plate, something that expresses their sameness and closeness.

7.2.2 Feeding As a Transaction (Transactional Dimension)

In Taiwan and Madagascar, the transactional dimension of feeding is particularly pronounced, while the proximal dimension is rather confined. In both settings, prolonged hand-feeding as it is practiced in Sri Lanka would be evaluated as a violation of the norms of intergenerational physical distancing. Whereas feeding in a proximal sense ends in early childhood, feeding in a transactional meaning retains an important socio-emotional role throughout childhood and even into adulthood. In both settings, children learn that the food they eat is a gift from their parents, ancestors, and – in the Taiwanese case – also other spiritual beings. Even though adults produce their own food, they can only do so as they receive ancestral blessing. In Taiwan, this blessing keeps the fields fertile and protects people from devastating typhoons. In Madagascar, it allows the cattle to thrive and is needed to keep humans alive and healthy. The benevolence of the ancestors has to be reciprocated by obedience, gratitude, and respect as well as by sacrificial offerings.

However, the socio-emotional significance of food transactions is emphasized somewhat differently in the two settings: In Madagascar, the transactional dimension is introduced through a distinct body-centered form of care and extensive breastfeeding, which is also used as prime means to calm infants and toddlers. With weaning, the exclusive bond between mother and child is understood to diminish as others become feeders as well. Older children and adults experience the transactional dimension mainly through its disruption: Disobedient children may be excluded from meals, and adults who transgressed moral norms must fear that their elders or ancestors will cease to provide them with the life force necessary to produce food and to sustain their own life. Thus, intergenerational relationships are so closely entwined with the transaction of food, or its abstract form of life force, that a rupture in these relationships is believed to potentially lead to death. These instances of social ruptures and associated fears are, however, exceptional and underline the normal condition in which the individual can rely on a constant influx of food and life force from the parents and ancestors.

In Taiwan, the socio-emotional significance of food transactions is also experienced through disruptions, but these are ascribed to a dangerous environment inhabited with malicious spirits. If people break the ancestral taboos, their ancestors turn away from them in aversion and contempt as they cannot bear human misconduct. Without ancestral protection, malicious spirits destroy the human livelihood and possess people's bodies. For this reason, Taiwanese children do not so much fear their enraged parents and immediate ancestors, as it is the case in Madagascar, but rather experience a diffuse form of anxiety, which is connected to an unreliable and sometimes hostile environment. In this context, children and adults experience the food they receive from parents and ancestors as a source of security that cannot be taken for granted. Thus, the provision of food itself is perceived as an act of love and affection that elicits feelings of joy and gratitude.

In both societies, the intergenerational transaction of food and life-sustaining blessing fosters hierarchical relationships that are organized in unidirectional ways. Juniors are expected to return obedience, deference, and gratitude but not food and knowledge as this would be in opposition to the general principles of life.

As with proximal feeding in Sri Lanka, transactional feeding also occurs in egalitarian relationships. In Taiwan and Madagascar, relationships between individuals and members of the same generation are viewed as equals. From an early age onward, children spend most of their time playing with peers. In Madagascar, they spend a considerable part of the day searching for wild foods or hunting for small animals, which they share or exchange among friends. If Taiwanese children of the same age do not share food, they are bullied by their peers. Furthermore, in this setting, related households are obliged to exchange food regularly with each other. If they fail to do so, kinship relations come to an end.

The transactional dimension is relevant in some of the other settings as well.[12] One place to see this is in the practice of *milk kinship*, which in some rare cases is still being practiced in Morocco but existed formerly also in Sri Lanka and Taiwan. Milk kinship is a relationship developed through the breast-feeding of an infant by several "mothers" or by someone other than the birth

---

[12] Mealtime prayers among Christian families are another practical example of transactional feeding and eating since meals are framed as gifts of God.

mother. Intergenerational relationships in these settings have been constituted by the giving of milk. Children, who have been nourished in this way may have the obligation to repay their "milk mothers" by assisting them in old age.

7.2.3 Feeding As a Prime Occasion for Sociality (Distal Dimension)

The *distal* dimension of feeding is most strongly pronounced in the examples from Costa Rica and Morocco. Most middle-class parents in Costa Rica believe that breastfeeding contributes importantly to mother–child attachments. However, rather than the transfer of substances or the act of feeding in itself, they emphasize co-occurring interactions as decisive for bonding: intensive moments of closeness, of having eye contact, engaging in baby talk, and exchanging positive emotions. For this purpose, mothers usually withdraw to calm and comfortable spaces for breastfeeding. This is in stark contrast to mothers in Madagascar, who rarely interrupt ongoing activities and usually do not exclusively focus on their children while breastfeeding. After Costa Rican children have been weaned, the emphasis on feeding and eating as occasions for conviviality is continued in the larger circle of extended family meals, which are considered crucial family events. In Morocco, mealtimes are also elaborated as important occasions for regular, extended family gatherings. Those who eat together are received as kin. Commensality and conviviality are inextricably blended, with neither activity more important than the other.

In both Costa Rica and Morocco, feeding and eating are associated with positive emotionality. The atmosphere of mealtime gatherings in Morocco is lively, warm, and relaxing. Family members frequently kiss and cuddle children or play with them during these occasions. Thus, infants and toddlers experience feelings of affection, warmth, and belonging while being fed and participating in mealtimes. By regularly eating together with extended family members, they develop a sense of the family as a place of safety and well-being. In Costa Rica, young children are encouraged and praised if they try foods that are viewed as healthy. Caregivers encourage playful explorations of food, a behavior that is frowned upon in Taiwan for instance.

In contrast to the proximal and transactional dimensions that imply unequal roles of providing and receiving, at least in caregiver–child relationships, the distal dimension tends to promote egalitarian relationships as it allows for symmetric, reciprocal interaction – for example, through eye contact or the joint participation in family meals. In Costa Rica, this egalitarian aspect is particularly emphasized in caregiver–child interactions, while Moroccan children experience an egalitarian aspect of social relationships through connections with extended family and guests.

It is important to note, however, that mealtimes in Costa Rica and in Morocco are also important occasions for teaching and disciplining. Children in Morocco have to wait patiently until mothers provide the desired food and may experience corporal punishment during mealtimes. In Costa Rica, children are expected to learn table manners and respectful behavior according to traditional values of *familismo*. Therefore, family meals in these settings may also serve as occasions for practicing hierarchical relationships.

The distal dimension of feeding is significantly less emphasized in the Malagasy and Taiwanese cases, where even the equalizing tendency of commensality may be minimized or counterbalanced, for example when women and men eat separately or when co-eaters begin and end eating in a status-dependent sequence. As we have demonstrated in this section, there are at least three ways of how feeding can contribute to relationship formation. Furthermore, our examples show that each of the three socio-emotional dimensions of feeding may be elaborated differently.

7.3 Four Claims and Some Theoretical Implications

The ethnographic case studies and subsequent analysis presented thus far lead us to make four claims that contradict or substantially expand attachment theory and the doctrine of sensitive responsiveness in their current forms: *First, there is no universally optimal way of feeding*. In most of our settings, feeding practices depart clearly from the norms of responsive feeding. These differences cannot be explained by lack of parental knowledge or skills, as the pediatric literature would have it. To the contrary, the differences are rooted in particular understandings of food and its role in social relationships that deviate from Euro-American middle-class norms. Furthermore, the observation that feeding practices vary widely across the five settings demonstrates how misleading it would be to classify them solely along a dichotomy of responsive versus nonresponsive feeding.

Second, feeding may play a crucial role in human bonding. In all five settings, feeding contributes in fundamental ways to the formation and maintenance of attachments, intergenerational relationships, and belonging. This is not to say that the attachment function of feeding is universal, nor that it is necessarily required for the development of social bonds; however, our cases as well as the broader ethnographic record demonstrate that this function is widespread, indicating that the disregard of feeding in attachment theory may reflect its origins in a highly specific historical, intellectual, and cultural context. Attachment theorists have to recognize that feeding as well as other body-centered caregiving practices are crucial for relationship formation in many parts of the world.

Third, feeding contributes to human bonding through different socio-emotional dimensions. Among our cases, we identified three socio-emotional dimensions of feeding, which we have labeled proximal, transactional, and distal. While in the proximal and distal dimensions ideally positive emotions are exchanged between children and caregivers, it is the absence of disruption, or of anxiety and fear, that is experienced as a wishful normality in the transactional dimension. At the core of the intergenerational feeding relationships described in the five settings, we find feelings of security and being cared for, whether they are based on physical closeness and trust, respect and gratitude, or the closeness of psychic-emotional intimacy. These feelings may become associated with and reproduced through various aspects of feeding – the physical intimate feeding interaction (proximal), receiving food as a life-sustaining gift (transactional), and conviviality in the context of regular meals (distal). Therefore, it can be stated that different modes of intergenerational feeding foster different forms of attachment between children and caregivers and that the relationships expressed through them are endowed with culturally specific meanings. From this, it follows that the quality of bonding relationships cannot simply be evaluated on a universal scale as it is practiced by attachment theorists who use the terms "secure," "avoidant," and "disorganized" to classify good and bad styles of mother–child interactions.

The concept of attachment security as described in attachment theory, namely that children feel close to and protected by their main caregivers and rely on them as a "safe haven" in situations of stress, may be just one of several understandings of attachment security. What poses a serious "risk" to a child's physical and/or psychological well-being and how a "secure" relationship is being established is evaluated and defined differently in each of the three sociocultural dimensions. Furthermore, feeding practices play an important role in the formation of culturally specific "socializing emotions" (e.g., pride, shame, anxiety, and fear; see Röttger-Rössler et al., 2015) and, thus, in the shaping of socio-emotional developmental pathways.

Fourth, feeding contributes to different forms of relationships. Through feeding and eating interactions, caregivers in our research sites express important core values about how different generations should relate to each other. In all five settings, we find either a mix of egalitarian and hierarchical orientations within intergenerational relationships (Costa Rica and Morocco) or predominantly hierarchical orientations within caregiver–child relationships, which are complemented by egalitarian peer relations (Sri Lanka, Madagascar, and Taiwan). In the latter cases, egalitarian intergenerational feeding relationships – as proposed by attachment theory and related approaches – simply would not make sense, as this would upend the established social, moral, and even supernatural orders on which these societies are grounded. Feeding practices are deeply embedded in the wider ecological, religious, socioeconomic, and polit- ico-historical context and cannot be treated as mere side aspects of social life. Therefore, attachment theory needs to include hierarchical models of caregiver– child relationships in its theorizing and to recognize that in many (if not most) settings across the globe hierarchical relationships are not viewed as something bad that hinders healthy child development.

7.4 The Emotional Turn and the Emergence of Attachment Theory

The importance of feeding for relationship formation is so obvious in our five research settings that one can only wonder why attachment theory missed this point. This astonishing neglect might be partly explained by the specific histor- ical, geographical, and sociocultural contexts from which attachment theory emerged as well as the disciplinary divisions on which its theorizing was and still is based. Attachment theory came into being as part of a broader emotional turn that took place in the 1930s and 1940s in the US East Coast, moving away from both popular understandings and psychological theories in early twenti- eth-century Europe and the United States that prioritized body-centered care for children's well-being and healthy development (Vicedo, 2014). Exemplifying this focus on children's emotions over bodily needs, the founder of attachment theory, John Bowlby, writes, "The young child's hunger for his mother's love and presence is greater as his hunger for food" (Bowlby, 1969, xiii). He derived his claims from research in foundling homes in which children, in spite of receiving sufficient material and physical care, literally withered away as they did not have loving mothers at their sides (Vicedo, 2014, p. 28).[13]

Bowlby and other influential psychiatrists of his time adhered to a strict division between the psychological and physiological aspects of life. They saw themselves as primarily responsible for the mental health of their young patients, which they separated from physical well-being. Already shortly after World War II, Bowlby believed that economic, nutritional, medical, and hous- ing difficulties had sufficiently been solved. He turned his focus to emotional instability and parents who lacked the ability to attune in adequate ways to the psychic-emotional needs of their children (Holmes, 2014). It was the psyche that needed to be fixed in order to overcome the troubles of war and to develop a better and more peaceful society (Bowlby, 1952; see also Vicedo, 2014).

---

[13] Interestingly, this situation was not dissimilar to Bowlby's own upbringing in an emotionally distant family that left childcare to a nanny and put him in a boarding school at an early age, practices that were quite common in British upper-middle-class families in the first half of the twentieth century (Holmes, 2014; Vicedo, 2014).

The neglect of feeding in attachment theory can be further explained by Bowlby's close personal and scientific contact with Harry Harlow, an American experimental psychologist who conducted experiments on rhesus monkey infants. In these experiments, the monkeys were isolated and given the choice to interact with two surrogate "mothers": one made of bare wire and holding food and one made of cloth but holding nothing. The monkeys overwhelmingly preferred the cloth mother and only went to the wire mother when they were hungry. From this, Bowlby and Harlow concluded that clinging, rather than feeding, was an evolutionary primary response in higher mammals and humans (Bowlby 1958, p. 366; Harlow 1958). Bowlby, who lacked empirical evidence for his new theory, highly profited from Harlow's experiments, for which he in turn gave important theoretical impulses (Van der Horst et al., 2008). Harlow later distanced himself from Bowlby's view about the key role of the mother in infant development as his experiments went on and he became aware of the importance of peers relations. Harlow's explorations from rhesus monkeys to humans proved controversial and were assessed differently in the various disciplines (Vicedo, 2014, p. 178).

A different perspective on the role of feeding for attachment formation was initially taken by Mary Ainsworth, the cofounder of attachment theory, who conducted research in Uganda in 1954. Based on this research, she stated that feeding may become a crucial dimension of attachments (Ainsworth, 1977). However, this hint was not pursued further in the subsequent, Western-dominated research.

7.5 Rediscovering Body-Centered Practices

In attachment theory, children mainly consist of minds, as this is the place where their emotions, psychological needs, and subjective preferences are located. That children also need a well-nourished body to live and thrive was obscured, a position that has not changed. The *Handbook of Attachment* proclaims that caregiving is a subordinated psychological system with the primary aim of establishing an optimal balance between attachment and exploration behaviors of young children (Feeney & Woodhouse, 2016). Contemporary attachment theorists do not question Bowlby's view that "secure attachment" between mother and child ultimately derives from an adequate maternal regulation of anxiety and fear. "Sensitive" and "responsive" mothers are seen as a "secure haven" for their children, a retreat to which children can always return from playful explorations when experiencing danger, irritation, and frustration (Bowlby, 1958, 1969). The regulation of young children's distress and the exchange of positive emotions are seen as more important than body-centered caregiving like feeding, which can only play a subordinate role in attachment formation in as much as they contribute to the pleasant emotional atmospheres between mothers and children that facilitate bonding.

There are, however, some voices from cultural psychology, social and cultural anthropology (Morelli et al., 2017), sociology (Bell, 2009, 2010, 2012), evolutionary psychology (MacDonald, 1992, 1999), and neuroscience (Sheridian & Bard, 2017) who claim that there are no scientific justifications why affective bonds between caregivers and children should not be related to body-centered caregiving. They argue that parents' interest in the well-being of their children cannot be reduced to healthy psychological development alone but must also include protection from physical dangers such as hunger and diseases.

As the evidence we have presented demonstrates, body-centered caregiving practices like feeding should be viewed as potentially equally important for attachment formation as the distal socialization practices recommended by attachment theory. Moreover, developmental psychologists and pediatrics should be aware of the possibility that the Western middle-class model of relationship formation on which attachment theory rests does not resemble human bonding in the majority of the world and should be viewed as a special case (Henrich et al., 2010). Our own research and analysis as well as a growing number of publications from social and cultural anthropology point toward this direction. Attachment theory needs to be freed from its contextual constraints to transform it into a truly universal theory with multiple approaches. We believe that an inclusion of body-centered caregiving practices in its theorizing would be a good starting point.

8 Conclusions, Implications, and the Politics of Feeding Children

Universal standards of children's development and care draw inspiration from "standardized" research in developmental psychology and medicine. Responsive, sensitive caregiving in nuclear family settings through face-to-face, playful, and predominantly verbal interactions between a primary caregiver and child are assumed to be the optimal conditions for developmental outcomes (Keller & Chaudhary, 2017). Whether for parents seeking advice about childcare, promoting welfare activities among marginalized groups, or establishing standards of health and well-being, this model has gained acceptance among practitioners worldwide. Any departures from these "gold standards" are evaluated as unfavorable for children.

While these standards are deployed to enforce particular ways of raising children within communities around the world, these have particular force as they are tied to international aid. Rooted in colonization, imagined binaries like North and South, East and West, Rich and Poor facilitate the flow of ideas in one direction – wealth to poverty – and movement of people in reverse – poverty to wealth (Appadurai, 1990; Therien, 2010).

Policy and programs for family interventions have a major presence in the Global South.[14] A prominent argument among international aid agencies is that poverty prevails in these countries because of poor parenting that prevents children from reaching their developmental potential, resulting in an estimated "20% loss in productivity" (WHO & UNICEF, 2012a). In the Nurturing Care Framework as well as the Care for Child Development (CCD) Package the emphasis is clear: "These disadvantaged children do poorly in school and subsequently have low incomes, high fertility, high criminality, and provide poor care for their own children" (WHO & UNICEF, 2012b). If parents are trained in responsive caregiving, they will allegedly thrive, and families will prosper. Although cultural conditions are a result of structural, ecological, and to some extent behavioral causes, the current view attributes disadvantage primarily to behavioral antecedents while ignoring others (Wacquant, 2022). These arguments are used to justify interventions that target childcare practices.

8.1 Responsive Feeding: Brief History and Overview

In the current literature, responsive feeding is described as a form of responsive parenting and, thus, as aligned to attachment theory. Accordingly, responsive feeding is understood as a reciprocal interaction between parent and child in which the parent creates a routine of meals, attends in a sensitive manner to the child's signals of hunger and satiety, and responds in a prompt, emotionally supportive, contingent, and developmentally appropriate way. These definitions of responsive feeding guide interventions aimed at changing feeding behaviors so that they include these reciprocal interactions in four stages:

(1) The child signals hunger or satiety through actions and expressions;
(2) The caregiver recognizes the cues;
(3) The caregiver's response is prompt, nurturing, and developmentally appropriate; and,
(4) The child experiences the caregiver's response (Garg et al., 2020).

---

[14] The divisions in power and access between countries and populations are hard to name but easy to see. The term "Global South" was intended as a "value-free" alternative to prior efforts to identify this divide in terms like "third-world," "poor," or "underdeveloped." Whether in Africa, Asia, or Latin America, the countries of the Global South have all been former colonies or they still are, dominated by powers in the Global North (for further discussions, see Appadurai, 1990 and Litonjua, 2012).

Further, it is argued:

> Responsive feeding helps children develop self-regulation over food intake and facilitates their transition to eating independently. Social interactions between caregivers and children such as speaking to the child, singing, and encouraging them also stimulate connections in the child's brain and promote cognitive development. Several studies have shown a positive association between responsive feeding and improved child nutrition. Responsive feeding practices, where caregivers interact with children and respond to their hunger and satiety cues, have been found to improve children's acceptance of food and adequate food intake. (Garg et al., 2020, p. 17)

Beginning around the year 2000, the principles of responsive feeding have been increasingly included in the policies of organizations working in countries of the Global South. A milestone within this process was the incorporation of responsive feeding in the WHO and UNICEF's Global Strategy for Infant and Young Child Feeding, which appeared in 2003. Now responsive feeding is promoted as part of programs at UNICEF and WHO, such as Facts for Life or Care for Child Development, and other organizations, like Save the Children. Responsive feeding interventions are in place all over the world, particularly in rural communities. The Infant and Young Feeding Counseling of WHO and UNICEF (2006) may serve as an example of how the concept of responsive feeding is applied in more concrete terms. As part of responsive feeding trainings, the participants are asked to play and discuss the three episodes given in Figure 5.

Ethnographic studies also demonstrate the imposition of these recommendations. For instance, in Costa Rica policies attempt to intervene in parenting behavior in line with universal feeding guidelines. After giving birth, all mothers are taught in the hospital how to breastfeed their babies exclusively for the first six months. For this purpose, the government has integrated so-called breastfeeding clinics in most hospitals (Ministerio de Salud, 2012). Traditional feeding of, for example, mashed plantains or chamomile tea from three to four months is strictly forbidden. From six months, parents are advised by pediatricians to let children explore specific foods. Many middle-class parents attend extra classes from organizations like La Leche League to learn "baby-led weaning" techniques. Parents report feeling a lot of social pressure and quickly become distressed when breastfeeding does not work out as expected.

In the Taiwanese setting, Han-Taiwanese school teachers try to correct the parenting styles of Indigenous Tao parents, which are believed to lack the characteristics of responsive caregiving. For instance, parents are told to create valuable moments of emotional intimacy by reading storybooks to their children or by playing with them. In addition, parents are advised to praise their

---

DEMONSTRATION 34.A CONTROLLED FEEDING

The 'young child' is sitting next to the caregiver (or on the caregiver's knees). The caretaker prevents the child from putting his/her hands near the bowl or the food.

The caregiver spoons food into the child's mouth.
If the child struggles or turns away, he is brought back to the feeding position.
Child may be slapped or forced if he does not eat.
The caregiver decides when the child has eaten enough and takes the bowl away.

DEMONSTRATION 34.B LEAVE TO THEMSELVES

The 'young child' on the floor sitting on a mat.
Caregiver puts a bowl of food beside the child with a spoon in it.
Caregiver turns away and continues with other activities (nothing too distracting for those watching).
Caregiver does not make eye contact with the child or help very much with feeding.
Child pushes food around the bowl, looks to caregiver for help, eats a little, cannot manage a spoon well, he tries with his hands but drops the food, he gives up and moves away.
Caregiver says, "Oh, you aren't hungry" and takes the bowl away.

DEMONSTRATION 34.C RESPONSIVE FEEDING

Caregiver washes the child's hands and her own hands and then sits level with child. Caregiver keeps eye contact and smiles at child. Using a small spoon and an individual bowl, small amounts of food are put to the child's lips and child opens his mouth and takes it a few times.

Caregiver praises child and makes pleasant comments – "Aren't you a good boy", "Here is lovely dinner" while feeding slowly.
Child stops taking food by shutting mouth or turning away. Caregiver tries once – "Another spoonful of lovely dinner?" Child refuses and caregiver stops feeding.

Caregiver offers a piece of food that child can hold - bread crust, biscuit or something similar. "Would you like to feed yourself?" Child takes it, smiles and sucks/munches it.
Caregiver encourages "You want to feed yourself, do you?"
After a minute, the caregiver offers a bit more from the bowl. Child starts taking spoonfuls again.

Figure 5 Interpretations of inappropriate (34.A, 34.B) and recommended (34.C) feeding styles by WHO and UNICEF (2006, pp. 456–458).
© the coauthors

children for little achievements and to generate a stress-free and happy atmosphere at home. Although teachers have good intentions and want to support their students' educational success, they completely miss that the suggested behaviors contradict important social norms and cultural values in this local setting (Funk, 2022).

Evidence of the spread of policies based on global recommendations by WHO and UNICEF is also seen in India where strategic action is ongoing to introduce interventions at multiple levels: the family, community, healthcare providers, and government. In one example, a leading panel of doctors at the Indian Academy of Pediatrics argued for the promotion of "responsive care" as the answer to problems related to health care and parenting in Indian families. "Barriers like inadequate sensitization of the community and low competency of health care providers need to be overcome. IAP (Indian Academy of Pediatrics) firmly believes that responsive parenting interventions revolving around nurturing care should be incorporated in office practice" (Mukherjee et al., 2021, p. 962). Apart from the direct contribution of funds for food programs, international NGOs have intensified the movement toward influencing behavioral change in countries like India through the establishment of multiple task forces (Sharma et al., 2022). This presents a clear shift from earlier interventions through supplementary feeding programs that provided direct food aid to children, usually at early childcare centers and schools, to interventions focused on behavioral change in feeding practices at home, what is labeled as complementary feeding under the Nurturing Care Framework (Garg et al., 2020).

8.2 Challenging Nurturing Care Framework and Responsive Feeding Interventions: Lessons from the Field

The concept of responsive caregiving has been established as a globally applied parenting standard through the Nurturing Care Framework (WHO et al., 2018), guiding recommendations about optimal care. In line with our earlier descriptions, responsive feeding promotes specific relational orientations toward children that should be dyadic, face-to-face, responsive, warm, and interactive. The overriding principle is that the consumption of food is an individual, self-regulated activity in which caregivers are temporary facilitators. However, the ways that children are fed around the world, as this Element demonstrates, vary widely from this singular model whose explanatory force is mainly confined to Euro-American middle-class settings.

Our central thesis is that feeding and food sharing are key experiences among human societies, closely managed through childhood to foster security, affection, sustenance, and a sense of belonging. This collection of ethnographic studies demonstrates that feeding is intimately tied to the cultural value systems in each community and that the developmental significance of food sharing lies at the core of children's care. Taken together, these studies on feeding practices provide ample material to question the contemporary understanding of childhood care and development, particularly the psychological and pediatric research that dominates expert understandings of childcare and development worldwide. As we discussed in the introduction, interventions in early childhood are guided by principles constructed around a narrow range of studies and fail to acknowledge cultural differences as well as the centrality of everyday practices like feeding, where children's development and journey to adulthood are socially and emotionally meaningful (Quinn, 2005).

8.3 Challenges to Universalization

This Element provides four major challenges to the universal imposition of contemporary Western-influenced childcare standards. *First, knowledge about diversity in contexts of childhood is grossly inadequate.* Drawing from feeding and related care practices in five settings illustrates just a small sample of worldwide diversity; and yet, we find important differences from the mainstream model. Furthermore, each community has a unique organization of feeding arrangements and activities that make them distinct. Children grow up with widely different material, ecological, social, and spiritual resources. From the food and feeding arrangements, feeding through the life course, and modes of interaction during feeding, children experience diverse conditions, practices, and value orientations. Further, the nuclear family is not the only setting in which children develop. A wide variety of people participate in children's care, adults and children, family members, and others. According to mainstream developmental psychology, a nuclear family with a dedicated primary caregiver and a small number of children is assumed to be the most favorable setting for optimal child development. Because of this limited perspective that is based on recent historical changes in family life in affluent countries (Brooks, 2020; Henrich, 2020), policy and practice in fields like nutrition, health care, and education are centered around the idea of "parenting," especially focusing on the mother. However, the five ethnographic reports in this Element reflect different types of family arrangements and the involvement of several social others, including adult caregivers from the extended family, elder siblings and cousins, and even ancestors.

Second, there is a failure of existing methods to capture the experiences and outcomes of children's development in different environments. Tools and measures commonly used for assessment of children derive from mainstream developmental psychology. Because of the focus on individual performance, children growing up in multiple-generation families, rural environments, or other family settings systematically underperform (Chaudhary, 2008). Popular methods of observation or assessment have expectations like exclusive attention, undisturbed circumstances, and familiarity with individual testing. Based on the evidence provided, such assessment tools or methods that fail to account for the cultural conditions cannot claim ecological validity. By using methods that closely examine everyday practices through immersed observations and interviews, these studies have captured dimensions of feeding and related childcare routines that facilitate in-depth cultural understanding. Through these methods, they are able to explore underlying beliefs that demonstrate the reasoning and significance of the respective cultural solutions to everyday tasks of feeding children and the deep psychological, social, and emotional significance of feeding in the early socialization of children.

Third, based on the findings of these studies, *it is abundantly clear that everyday activities like feeding are central to cultural meaning systems*. Each cultural context was found to have unique features that have social and historic significance. Far from being marginal to the formation of social and emotional experiences, in these examples we find that feeding lies at the heart of a child's entry into a social world. As we have illustrated, the people in our research sites, for various reasons, stress the importance of feeding for relationship formation and maintenance. Intergenerational feeding is a core expression of central sociocultural values and meanings – what we might call *familismo* in Costa Rica, a blend of conviviality and commensality central to kinship in Morocco, a cultural model for hierarchical relationships in Sri Lanka, and a sharing of substances through the benevolence of ancestors and other spiritual beings in Madagascar and Taiwan.

Fourth, these accounts are a direct challenge to the assumption that food consumption is an individual achievement in which adults are simply facilitators. In each of the contexts studied, feeding is central to the social relationships and value orientations and cannot be viewed as an individual activity – even when people eat alone. Despite this, the objective of self-reliance is evident in each community, albeit in different ways. The assumption that extended, adult-led feeding is harmful is not evident. Attributing neglect, force, or abuse to cultural practices in feeding children is unfair and unjustified. Rather, adult-led feeding can be perceived as a caring act within a hierarchical cultural framework in which the lives of children and caregivers are connected through mutual obligations. If we remove the dichotomy of self-feeding versus force-feeding, there are a range of possibilities that emerge, all of which relate to social-emotional values held by people. The focus on becoming independent in eating is an important objective of the responsive and sensitive feeding paradigm, and several strategies are advised to assist children to become self-reliant in feeding. Each community brings its best beliefs forward as they care for their children, making choices in the arrangements. As we have learned from the work of Kağıtçıbaşı (2005) and Keller (2007), autonomy and relatedness are not mutually exclusive as is often assumed in Western scholarship.

Without addressing these four challenges, the sciences that promote current global standards cannot adequately understand or explain feeding routines in diverse cultural settings. When we take the insider view, the sense-making and cultural value of these practices become evident. The ethnographies in this Element present a direct challenge to scientific evidence based on narrow samples of idealized Western middle-class parents that fail to represent the diversity even within the "West." Family interventions that attempt to change local care practices do not acknowledge, accept, and understand their significance in the cultural project of children's development. Furthermore, we argue that intervening with local childcare solutions such as feeding practices can create unforeseen challenges and violate people's inalienable rights to bring up their children in their own way.

Scholarly work in the fields of anthropology, sociology, and cultural and critical psychology that delves deeply into cultural dynamics, social processes, and ecological settings has repeatedly demonstrated that there is no universally ideal childhood. Yet global agencies persist in the promotion of a narrow set of standards in care, completely ignoring this literature (Chaudhary, 2021). The creation of global standards and their worldwide implementation is based on specific theoretical and methodological traditions, while others are being ignored. Global intervention programs are rooted in a history of economic inequality and international dominance. As these ethnographic examples have demonstrated, families live with local cultural practices that have emerged over generations under specific ecological conditions. These practices are valued and justified as strategies to guide children to becoming valued members of family and larger society. The cherry-picking of "evidence-based" research that collapses diversity to promote WEIRD science is unjust since any digression from this vision is deemed deficient or defective.

The imposition of feeding interventions and other ways of raising children takes place both within and across cultures to impose the norms of affluent societies, both within countries (as in the case of ethnic minorities, immigrants, and disadvantaged communities) and across nations (through international aid and welfare activities). Such campaigns have been achieved by priming practices based on a narrow ideology while vilifying practices of the majority world and people who live with relative poverty and ideological difference. Given the ethnographic evidence emerging from this Element, such interventions can be judged as promoting epistemic violence in addition to bad science.[15] Food-related interventions interfere not only in the amount of food available to the child but also in the kind of food materials that are eaten, the sentiments attached to feeding, and the other "gastro-semantic" experiences and meaning associations that include a culture's "distinct capacity to signify, experience, systematise, philosophise and communicate with food" (Khare, 1992, p. 44). The shift from evidence-based practices to ethics-based interventions is thus an urgent call (Knizek & Klempe, 2021), and one that requires dense ethnographic descriptions.

---

[15] "Epistemic violence" refers to harm inflicted on people through discourse (Spivak, 1988) and the systematic suppression of diversity in everyday experiences.

The close ethnography presented in this Element demonstrates that the idea of simply changing specific caregiving practices like feeding to "improve" developmental outcomes is deeply problematic. These practices connect people to their ecological and social contexts in intimate ways; one cannot simply change one aspect of childcare without transforming a much larger value system. Whether it concerns autonomy or relatedness, hierarchical or egalitarian relationships, care by one or many, feeding practices are deeply embedded in the ecological, religious, socioeconomic, and political-historic contexts. These cultural practices cannot be treated as marginal or separate from cultural meaning systems.

By choosing intergenerational feeding relationships as the focus of our Element, we are able to demonstrate that attachment formation across the world is much more diverse than currently acknowledged in mainstream developmental sciences. Any theory of human bonding has to take into account that there is no universal setup for relationship formation but a multitude of culturally distinct socio-emotional pathways. We believe that sensitive responsiveness as a particular interaction style and feeding as a body-centered care practice are only two out of several possible ways of attachment formation. Our Element suggests that research and theorizing about bonding and relationship formation needs to fully account for this variability in order to become universally valid rather than claiming universal validity for a specific form of attachment formation. Our Element also has important practical and political implications, since globally applied feeding interventions and other early childhood programs are still grounded on hegemonial discourses about relationship formation that are themselves based on classical attachment theory and related approaches. In order to prevent new forms of cultural imperialisms of unprecedented scope, we need to stretch our culture-bound theories of development to become more inclusive, more flexible, and more truly universal. For this effort to succeed, we need to cross disciplinary divides and oppose cultural chauvinism that prevent us from sharing research questions, approaches, findings, and theory-building. With this Element we hope to contribute to that cross-disciplinary conversation.

References

Aboud, F. E., Shafique, S., & Akhter, S. (2009). A Responsive Feeding Intervention Increases Children's Self-Feeding and Maternal Responsiveness but Not Weight Gain. *The Journal of Nutrition*, 139(9), 1738–1743.

Ainsworth, M. D. S. (1977). Infant Development and Mother–Infant Interaction among Ganda and American Families. In P. Herbert Leiderman, Steven R. Tulkin, & Anne Rosenfeld, eds., *Culture and Infancy: Variations in the Human Experience*. New York: Academic Press, pp. 119–149.

Appadurai, A. (1990). Disjuncture and Difference in the Global Cultural Economy. *Theory, Culture, & Society*, 7(2&3), 295–310. https://doi.org/10.1177/026327690007002017.

Barlow, K. (2013). Attachment and Culture in Murik Society: Learning Autonomy and Interdependence through Kinship, Food, and Gender. In N. Quinn & J. Mageo, eds., *Attachment Reconsidered Cultural Perspectives on a Western Theory*. New York: Springer, pp. 165–188.

Bell, D. (2009). Attachment without Fear. *Journal of Family Theory and Review*, 1(4), 177–197.

Bell, D. (2010). *The Dynamics of Connection: How Evolution and Biology Create Caregiving and Attachment*. Lanham, MD: Lexington Books.

Bell, D. (2012). Next Steps in Attachment Theory. *Journal of Family Theory and Review*, 4(4), 275–281.

Benedict, R. (1934). *Patterns of Culture*. Boston, MA: Houghton Mifflin.

Bentley, M. E., Wasser, H. M., & Creed-Kanashiro, H. M. (2011). Responsive Feeding and Child Undernutrition in Low- and Middle-Income Countries. *The Journal of Nutrition*, 141(3), 502–507.

Black, M. M., & Aboud, F. E. (2011). Responsive Feeding Is Embedded in a Theoretical Framework of Responsive Parenting. *The Journal of Nutrition*, 141(3), 490–494.

Bowlby, J. (1951). *Maternal Care and Mental Health*, Vol. 2. Geneva: World Health Organization.

Bowlby, J. (1952). Responses of Young Children to Separation from Their Mothers (with J. Robertson). *Courrier du Centre International de l'Enfance*, 2(2), 66–78, and 2(3), 131–142.

Bowlby, J. (1958). The Nature of the Child's Tie to His Mother. *International Journal of Psycho-Analysis*, 39, 350–373.

Bowlby, J. (1969). *Attachment and Loss, Vol. 1: Attachment*. New York: Basic Books.

Briggs, J. (1998). *Inuit Morality Play: The Emotional Education of a Three-Year-Old*. New Haven, CT: Yale University Press.

Brightman, M., Fausto, C., & Grotti, V. (2016). *Ownership and Nurture: Studies in Native Amazonian Property Relations*. New York: Berghahn Books.

Brooks, D. (2020). The Nuclear Family Was a Mistake. *The Atlantic*, March. www.theatlantic.com/magazine/archive/2020/03/the-nuclear-family-was-a-mistake/605536/.

Burman, E. ([1994] 2017). *Deconstructing Developmental Psychology*, 3rd ed. New York: Routledge.

Cantor, A., Peña, J., & Himmelgreen, D. (2013). "We Never Ate Like That, Not Fast Food, or Junk Foods": Accounts of Changing Maternal Diet in a Tourist Community in Rural Costa Rica. *Ecology of Food and Nutrition*, 52(6), 479–496.

Carsten, J. (1995). The Substance of Kinship and the Heat of the Hearth: Feeding, Personhood, and Relatedness among Malays in Pulau Langkawi. *American Ethnologist*, 22(2), 223–241.

Carsten, J. (1997). *The Heat of the Hearth: The Process of Kinship in a Fishing Community*. Oxford: Clarendon Press.

Carsten, J. (2000). *Cultures of Relatedness: New Approaches to the Study of Kinship*. Cambridge: Cambridge University Press.

Cassidy, J. (2016). The Nature of the Child's Tie. In J. Cassidy & P. R. Shaver, eds., *The Handbook of Attachment: Theory, Research, and Clinical Applications*. New York: Guilford Press, pp. 3–24.

Chapin, B. L. (2010). "We Have to Give": Sinhala Mothers' Responses to Children's Expressions of Desire. *Ethos*, 38(4), 354–368.

Chapin, B. L. (2013). Childcare, Dependency, and Autonomy in a Sri Lankan Village: Enculturation of and through Attachment Relationships. In N. Quinn & J. Mageo, eds., *Attachment Reconsidered: Cultural Perspectives on a Western Theory*. New York: Palgrave Macmillan, pp. 143–163.

Chapin, B. L. (2014). *Childhood in a Sri Lankan Village: Shaping Hierarchy and Desire*. New Brunswick, NJ: Rutgers University Press.

Chaudhary, N. (2004). *Listening to Culture: Constructing Reality from Everyday Talk*. New Delhi: Sage.

Chaudhary, N. (2008). Methods for a Cultural Science. In S. Anandalakshmy, N. Chaudhary, & N. Sharma, eds., *Researching Families and Children: Culturally Appropriate Methods*. New Delhi: Sage, pp. 29–52.

Chaudhary, N. (2020). The Science and Ethics of Intervention Programmes in Family and Child Welfare: Towards Building an Inclusive Psychology for Social Justice. *Human Arenas*, 3(2), 155–171.

Chaudhary, N. (2021). From Local Evidence to Global Science and Onward to Local Practice in a Post-Pandemic World: The Journey of Family Intervention Programs in India. In S. V. Klempe, O. V. Lehmann, & B. L. Knizek, eds., *Ethical Based Practices: A Theoretical Foundation*. New York: Springer, pp. 181–197.

Chaudhary, N., & Sriram, S. (2020). Psychology in the "Backyards of the World": Experiences from India. *Journal of Cross-Cultural Psychology*, 51(2), 113–133.

Costa, L. (2017). *The Owners of Kinship: Asymmetrical Relations in Indigenous Amazonia*. Chicago, IL: HAU Books.

Crittenden, P. M., & Clausen, A. H. (2000). *The Organization of Attachment Relationships: Maturation, Culture, and Context*. New York: Cambridge University Press.

De Jeude, M. V. L., Schütte, O., & Quesada, F. (2016). The Vicious Circle of Social Segregation and Spatial Fragmentation in Costa Rica's Greater Metropolitan Area. *Habitat International*, 54, 65–73.

Descola, P. (2013). *Beyond Nature and Culture*. Chicago, IL: Chicago University Press.

Dos Santos, G. D. (2009). The "Stove-Family" and the Process of Kinship in Rural South China. In S. Brandstätter & G. D. Dos Santos, eds., *Chinese Kinship: Contemporary Anthropological Perspectives*. London: Routledge, pp. 112–136.

Elli, L. (1993). *Une Civilisation du Bœuf: Les Bara de Madagascar. Difficultés et Perspectives d'une Évangélisation. [A Civilization Based on Cattle: The Bara of Madagascar. Difficulties and Perspectives of Evangelisation.]* Fianarantsoa: Ambozontany.

El Ouardani, C. (2014). Childhood and Development in Rural Morocco: Cultivating Reason and Strength. In D. Bowen, E. Early, & B. Schulthies, eds., *Everyday Life in the Muslim Middle East*, 3rd ed. Bloomington: Indiana University Press, pp. 24–38.

El Ouardani, C. (2018). Care of Neglect? Corporal Discipline Reform in a Rural Moroccan Classroom. *Anthropology and Education Quarterly*, 92(2), 129–145.

Engle, P. L., & Pelto, G. H. (2011). Responsive Feeding: Implications for Policy and Program Implementation. *The Journal of Nutrition*, 141(3), 508–511.

Ewing, K. P. (1991). Can Psychoanalytic Theories Explain the Pakistani Woman? Intrapsychic Autonomy and Interpersonal Engagement within the Family. *Ethos*, 19(2), 131–160.

Faircloth, C. (2013). *Militant Lactivism? Attachment Parenting and Intensive Motherhood in the UK and France*. Oxford: Berghahn Books.

Fallas Gamboa, K., & Solís Guillén, C. (2020). Características del Parentaje Intensivo en Familias Urbanas del Gran Area Metropolitana. [Characteristics of Intensive Parenting in Urban Families in the Greater Metropolitan Area.] Licentiate thesis. University of Costa Rica.

Faublée, J. (1954). *La Cohésion des Sociétés Bara.* [*Social Cohesion among the Bara.*] Paris: Presses Universitaires de France.

Feeney, B. C., & Woodhouse, S. S. (2016). Caregiving. In J. Cassidy & P. R. Shaver, eds., *Handbook of Attachment: Theory, Research, and Clinical Applications.* New York: Guilford Press, pp. 827–851.

Funk, L. (2014). Entanglements between Tao People and Anito on Lanyu Island, Taiwan. In Y. Musharbash & G.-H. Presterudstuen, eds., *Monster Anthropology in Australasia and Beyond.* New York: Palgrave Macmillan, pp. 143–157.

Funk, L. (2020). Bringing My Wife and Children to the Field: Methodological, Epistemological, and Ethical Reflections. In F. Braukmann, M. Haug, K. Metzmacher, & R. Stolz, eds., *Being a Parent in the Field: Implications and Challenges of Accompanied Fieldwork.* Bielefeld: Transcript, pp. 185–205.

Funk, L. (2022). *Geister der Kindheit: Sozialisation von Emotionen bei den Tao in Taiwan* [Ghosts of Childhood: Socialization of Emotions among the Tao in Taiwan]. Bielefeld: Transcript.

Funk, L., Röttger-Rössler, B., & Scheidecker, G. (2012). Fühlen(d) Lernen: Zur Sozialisation und Entwicklung von Emotionen im Kulturvergleich. [Learning (by) Feeling: On the Socialization and Development of Emotions in Cross-Cultural Comparison.] *Zeitschrift für Erziehungswissenschaften,* 16, 217–238.

Garg, A., Bégin, F., & Aguayo, V. (2020). *Improving Young Children's Diets during the Complementary Feeding Period.* New York: UNICEF. www.unicef.org/media/93981/file/Complementary-Feeding-Guidance-2020.pdf.

Gomez, M. S., Novaes, A. P. T., Silva, J. P. D., Guerra, L. M., & Possobon, R. D. F. (2020). Baby-Led Weaning, an Overview of the New Approach to Food Introduction: Integrative Literature Review. *Revista Paulista de Pediatria,* 38, e2018084.

Gottlieb, A. (2004). *The Afterlife Is Where We Come From: The Culture of Infancy in West Africa.* Chicago, IL: Chicago University Press.

Grusec, J. E., & Davidov, M. (2010). Integrating Different Perspectives on Socialization Theory and Research: A Domain-Specific Approach. *Child Development,* 81(3), 687–709.

Grusec, J. E., & Davidov, M. (2015). Analyzing Socialization from a Domain-Specific Perspective. In J. E. Grusec, ed., *Handbook of Socialization: Theory and Research.* New York: Guilford Press, pp. 285–319.

Hardman, C. (1973). Can There Be an Anthropology of Childhood? *Journal of the Anthropological Society of Oxford*, 8(4), 85–99.

Harlow, H. (1958). The Nature of Love. *American Psychologist*, 13(12), 673–685.

Henrich, J. (2020). *The Weirdest People in the World: How the West Became Psychologically Peculiar and Particularly Prosperous*. New York: Allen Lane.

Henrich, J., Heine, S. J., & Norenzayan, A. (2010). The Weirdest People in the World? *Behavioral and Brain Sciences*, 33(2–3), 61–83.

Hewlett, B. S. (1991). *Intimate Fathers*. Ann Arbor: University of Michigan Press.

Holmes, J. (2014). *John Bowlby and Attachment Theory*. New York: Routledge.

Huntington, R. (1988). *Gender and Social Structure in Madagascar*. Bloomington: Indiana University Press.

Janowski, M., & Kerlogue, F. (2007). *Kinship and Food in Southeast Asia*. Copenhagen: NIAS Press.

Kağıtçıbaşı, C. (2005). Autonomy and Relatedness in Cultural Context: Implications for Self and Family. *Journal of Cross-Cultural Psychology*, 36 (4), 404–422. https://doi.org/10.1177/0022022105275959.

Kakar, S. (1981). *The Inner World: The Psychoanalytic Study of Childhood and Society in India*. New Delhi: Oxford.

Keller, H. (2007). *Cultures of infancy*. Mahwah, NJ: Lawrence Erlbaum.

Keller, H. (2018). Universality Claim of Attachment Theory: Children's Socioemotional Development across Cultures. *Proceedings of the National Academy of Sciences of the United States of America*, 115(45), 11414–11419.

Keller, H., & Bard, K. A. (2017). *The Cultural Nature of Attachment: Contextualizing Relationships and Development*. Cambridge, MA: MIT Press.

Keller, H., & Chaudhary, N. (2017). Is the Mother Essential for Attachment? Models of Care in Different Cultures. In H. Keller & K. A. Bard, eds., *The Cultural Nature of Attachment: Contextualizing Relationships and Development*. Cambridge, MA: MIT Press, pp. 109–137.

Khare, R. S. (1992). *The Eternal Food: Gastronomic Ideas and Experiences of Hindus and Buddhists*. Albany: State University of New York Press.

Klein, J. A., Pottier, J., & West, H. G. (2012). New Directions in the Anthropology of Food. In R. Fardon, O. Harris, T. H. C. Marchand et al., eds., *The Sage Handbook of Social Anthropology*. London: Sage Publications, pp. 293–302.

Knizek, B. L., & Klempe, S. V. (2021). *Ethical Based Practices: A Theoretical Foundation*. Annals of Theoretical Psychology Series. New York: Springer.

Kusserow, A. (2004). *American Individualisms: Child Rearing and Social Class in Three Neighborhoods*. New York: Palgrave Macmillan.

Lachman, A., Berg, A., Ross, F., & Pentecost, M. (2021). Infant Mental Health in Southern Africa: Nurturing a Field. *The Lancet*, 398(10303), 835–836. https://doi.org/10.1016/S0140-6736(21)00998-3.

Lancy, D. F. (2007). Accounting for Variability in Mother–Child Play. *American Anthropologist*, 109(2), 273–284.

Lareau, A. (2003). *Unequal Childhoods: Class, Race, and Family Life*. Berkeley: University of California Press.

Latour, B. (1996). On Actor-Network Theory. A New Clarification Plus More Than a Few Complications. *Soziale Welt*, 47, 369–381.

Lee, E., Bristow, J., Faircloth, C. et al. (2014). *Parenting Culture Studies*. Basingstoke: Palgrave Macmillan.

LeVine, R. A. (2014). Attachment Theory As a Cultural Ideology. In H. Otto & H. Keller, eds., *Different Faces of Attachment: Cultural Variations on a Human Need*. Cambridge: Cambridge University Press, pp. 50–65.

LeVine, R. A., Dixon, S., LeVine, S. et al. (1994). *Child Care and Culture: Lessons from Africa*. Cambridge: Cambridge University Press.

LeVine, R. A., & LeVine, B. B. (1966). *Nyansongo: A Gusii Community in Kenya*. New York: Wiley.

LeVine, R. A., & LeVine, S. (2016). *Do Parents Matter? Why Japanese Babies Sleep Soundly, Mexican Siblings Don't Fight, and American Families Should Just Relax*. New York: PublicAffairs.

LeVine, R. A., & New, R. S (2008). *Anthropology and Child Development: A Cross-Cultural Reader*. Malden, MA: Blackwell Publishing.

LeVine, R., & Norman, K. (2001). The Infant's Acquisition of Culture: Early Attachment Reexamined in Anthropological Perspective. In C. C. Moore & H. F. Matthews, eds., *The Psychology of Cultural Experience*. New York: Cambridge University Press, pp. 83–103.

Levy, R. I. (1978). Tahitians: Gentleness and Redundant Controls. In A. Montagu, ed., *Learning Non-Aggression: The Experience of Non-Literate Societies*. Oxford: Oxford University Press, pp. 222–235.

Litonjua, M. D. (2012). Third World/Global South: From Modernization, to Dependency/ Liberation, to Postdevelopment. *Journal of Third World Studies*, 29(1), 25–57.

MacDonald, K. (1992). Warmth As Developmental Construction: An Evolutionary Analysis. *Child Development*, 63(4), 753–773.

MacDonald, K. (1999). Love and Confidence in Protection As Two Independent Systems Underlying Intimate Relationships. *Journal of Family Psychology*, 13(4), 492–495.

Mead, M. (1928). *Coming of Age in Samoa: A Study of Sex in Primitive Societies*. New York: William Morrow.

Mead, M. (1930). *Growing Up in New Guinea: A Comparative Study of Primitive Education*. New York: Morrow Quill Paperbacks.

Mead, M. (1954). Some Theoretical Considerations on the Problem of Mother–Child Separation. *American Journal of Orthopsychiatry*, 24(3), 471–483.

Mesman, J., Van Ijzendoorn, M. H., & Sagi-Schwartz, A. (2016). Cross-Cultural Patterns of Attachment: Universal and Contextual Dimensions. In J. Cassidy & P. R. Shaver, eds., *Handbook of Attachment: Theory, Research, and Clinical Applications*. New York: Guilford Press, pp. 852–877.

Ministerio de Salud (2009). *Política Pública de la Lactancia Materna*. [*Public Policy on Breastfeeding*.] https://siteal.iiep.unesco.org/bdnp/2224/politica-publica-lactancia-materna.

Ministerio de Salud (2012). *Manual Implementación Clínicas de Lactancia Materna y Desarrollo. Escenario Hospitalario*. [*Manual for the Implementation of Clinics for Breastfeeding and Development. Hospital Setting*.] www.binasss.sa.cr/manuallactancia.pdf.

Mintz, S. W., & Du Bois, C. M. (2002). The Anthropology of Food and Eating. *Annual Review of Anthropology*, 31, 99–119.

Morelli, G. A., Chaudhary, N., Gottlieb, A. et al. (2017). Taking Culture Seriously: A Pluralistic Approach to Attachment. In H. Keller & K. A. Bard, eds., *The Cultural Nature of Attachment: Contextualizing Relationships and Development*. Cambridge, MA: MIT Press, pp. 139–169.

Morelli, G. A., Quinn, N., Chaudhary, N. et al. (2018). Ethical Challenges of Parenting Interventions in Low- to Middle-Income Countries. *Journal of Cross-Cultural Psychology*, 49(1), 5–24.

Morris, A. S., Treat, A., Hays-Grudo, J. et al. (2018). Integrating Research and Theory on Early Relationships to Guide Intervention and Prevention. In A. S. Morris, ed., *Building Early Social and Emotional Relationships with Infants and Toddlers*. Cham: Springer, pp. 1–25.

Mukherjee, S. B., Agrawal, D., Mishra, D. et al. (2021). Indian Academy of Pediatrics Position Paper on Nurturing Care for Early Childhood Development. *Indian Pediatrics*, 58(10), 962–969.

Núñez Rivas, H. P., Campos Saborío, N., Alfaro Mora, F. V., & Holst Schumacher, I. (2013). Las Creencias sobre Obesidad de Niños y Niñas en Edad Escolar y las de sus Progenitores. [Beliefs about Obesity of School-Age Boys and Girls and Their Parents.] *Actualidades Investigativas en Educación*, 13(2), 1–30.

Ochs, E., & Kremer-Sadlik, T. (2015). How Postindustrial Families Talk. *Annual Review of Anthropology*, 44, 87–103.

Ochs, E., Pontecorvo, C., & Fasulo, A. (1996). Socializing Taste. *Ethnos*, 61 (1–2), 7–46.

Otto, H., & Keller, H. (2014). *Different Faces of Attachment: Cultural Variations on a Universal Human Need*. Cambridge: Cambridge University Press.

Pérez-Escamilla, R., Jimenez, E. Y., & Dewey, K. G. (2021). Responsive Feeding Recommendations: Harmonizing Integration into Dietary Guidelines for Infants and Young Children. *Current Developments in Nutrition*, 5(6), nzab076.

Prout, A., & James, A. (1997). A New Paradigm for the Sociology of Childhood? Provenance, Promise and Problems. In A. Prout & A. James, eds., *Constructing and Reconstructing Childhood: Contemporary Issues in the Sociological Study of Childhood*, 2nd ed. Bristol, PA: Falmer Press, pp. 7–32.

Quinn, N. (2005). Universals of Child Rearing. *Anthropological Theory*, 5(4), 477–516.

Quinn, N. (2013). Adult Attachment Cross-Culturally: A Reanalysis of the Ifaluk Emotion Fago. In N. Quinn & J. Mageo, eds., *Attachment Reconsidered: Cultural Perspectives on a Western Theory*. New York: Springer, pp. 215–239.

Quinn, N., & Mageo, J. (eds.) (2013). *Attachment Reconsidered: Cultural Perspectives on a Western Theory*. New York: Springer.

Rae-Espinoza, H. (2010). Consent and Discipline in Ecuador: How to Avoid Raising an Antisocial Child. *Ethos*, 38(4), 369–387.

Richards, A. I. ([1932] 2004). *Hunger and Work in a Savage Tribe: A Functional Study of Nutrition among the Southern Bantu*. New York: Routledge.

Ritchie, J., & Ritchie, J. (1979). *Growing Up in Polynesia*. Winchester, MA: Allen & Unwin.

Rosabal-Coto, M. (2012). Creencias y Prácticas de Crianza: El Estudio del Parentaje en el Contexto Costarricense. [Parenting Beliefs and Practices: The Study of Parenting in the Costa Rican Context.] *Revista Costarricense de Psicología*, 31(1–2), 65–100.

Rosabal-Coto, M., Quinn, N., Keller, H. et al. (2017). Real-World Applications to Attachment Theory. In H. Keller & K. A. Bard, eds., *The Cultural Nature of Attachment: Contextualizing Relationships and Development*. Cambridge, MA: MIT Press, pp. 335–354.

Röttger-Rössler, B. (2020). Research across Cultures and Disciplines: Methodological Challenges in an Interdisciplinary and Comparative

Research Project on Emotion Socialization. In M. Schnegg & E. D. Lowe, eds., *Comparing Cultures: Innovations in Comparative Ethnography*. Cambridge: Cambridge University Press, pp. 180–200.

Röttger-Rössler, B., Scheidecker, G., Jung, S., & Holodynski, M. (2013). Socializing Emotions in Childhood: A Cross-Cultural Comparison between the Bara in Madagascar and the Minangkabau in Indonesia. *Mind, Culture, and Activity*, 20(3), 260–287.

Röttger-Rössler, B., Scheidecker, G., Funk, L., & Holodynski, M. (2015). Learning (by) Feeling: A Cross-Cultural Comparison of the Socialization and Development of Emotions. *Ethos*, 43(2), 187–220.

Rozin, P. (2007). Food and Eating. In S. Kitayama & D. Cohen, eds., *Handbook of Cultural Psychology*. New York: Guilford Press, pp. 391–416.

Scheidecker, G. (2014). Cattle, Conflicts and Gendarmes in Southern Madagascar: A Local Perspective on *Fihavanana Gasy*. In P. Kneitz, ed., *Fihavanana – La Vision d'une Société en Paix à Madagascar. Perspectives Anthropologiques, Historiques et Socio-Économique*. Halle-Wittenberg: Universitätsverlag Halle-Wittenberg, pp. 129–156.

Scheidecker, G. (2017a). *Kindheit, Kultur und moralische Emotionen: Zur Sozialisation von Furcht und Wut im ländlichen Madagaskar* [*Childhood, Culture, and Moral Emotions. On the Socialization of Fear and Anger in Rural Madagascar*]. Bielefeld: Transcript.

Scheidecker, G. (2017b). Zwischen Angst und Empörung: Gendarmen und Gerechtigkeitsgefühle im rechtspluralen Kontext Madagaskars [Between Fear and Outrage: Gendarmes and Legal Sentiments in the Context of Legal Pluralism in Madagascar]. In J. Bens & O. Zenker, eds., *Gerechtigkeitsgefühle. Zur affektiven und emotionalen Legitimität von Normen*. Bielefeld: Transcript, pp. 73–103.

Scheidecker, G. (2020). Unfolding Emotions: The Language and Socialization of Anger in Madagascar. In S. E. Pritzker, J. Fenigsen, & J. H. Wilce, eds., *The Routledge Handbook of Languages and Emotion*. Abington: Routledge, pp. 49–70.

Scheidecker, G. (2023). Parents, Caregivers, and Peers: Patterns of Complementarity in the Social World of Children in Rural Madagascar. *Current Anthropology* 64(3).

Scheidecker, G., Chaudhary, N., Keller, H., Mezzenzana, F., & Lancy, D. (2023). "Poor Brain Development" in the Global South? Challenging the Science of Early Childhood Interventions. *Ethos*, 51(1), 3–26.

Scheidecker, G., Spallek, S., Tran, K. N., Geigenmüller, D., & Röttger-Rössler, B. (2021). Kultursensible sozialpädagogische Versorgung am Beispiel von Fütterstörungen. [Culturally Sensitive Social Pedagogical

Care for Feeding Disorders.] *Kinderärztliche Praxis: Sozialpädiatrie und Jugendmedizin*, 92(2), 98–102.

Schildkrout, E. (1978). Age and Gender in Hausa Society: Socio-Economic Roles of Children in Urban Kano. In J. La Fontaine, ed., *Sex and Age As Principles of Social Differentiation*. London: Academic Press, pp. 109–137.

Schmidt, W. J., Keller, H., & Rosabal-Coto, M. (2021). Development in Context: What We Need to Know to Assess Children's Attachment Relationships. *Developmental Psychology*, 57(12), 2206–2219.

Schmidt, W. J., Keller, H., & Rosabal-Coto, M. (2023a). The Cultural Specificity of Parent–Infant Interaction: Perspectives of Urban Middle-Class and Rural Indigenous Families in Costa Rica. *Personal Relationships*, 70, 101796.

Schmidt, W. J., Keller, H., Rosabal-Coto, M. et al. (2023b). Feeding, Food, and Attachment: An Underestimated Relationship? *Ethos*, 51(1), 62–80.

Sedó Masís, P., & Ureña Vargas, M. (2007). *Papel Social de las Abuelas en el Seno Familiar: Percepciones de un Grupo de Mujeres Mayores Residentes en Comunidades Urbanas de Costa Rica.* [*The Social Role of Grandmothers in the Family Unit: Perceptions of a Group of Elderly Women Residing in Urban Communities in Costa Rica.*] Research Report, Escuela de Nutrición, Costa Rica.

Seymour, S. C. (2013). "It Takes a Village to Raise a Child": Attachment Theory and Multiple Child Care in Alor, Indonesia and in North India. In N. Quinn & J. Mageo, eds., *Attachment Reconsidered: Cultural Perspectives on a Western Theory*. New York: Springer, pp. 115–139.

Sharma, M., Singh, T., Juneja, M. et al. (2022). Indian Academy of Pediatrics (IAP) Task Force Recommendations for Incorporating Nurturing Care for Early Childhood Development (NC-ECD) in Medical Education in India. *Indian Pediatrics*, 59(2), 137–141.

Sheridian, M. A., & Bard, K. A. (2017). Neural Consequences of Infant Attachment. In H. Keller & K. A. Bard, eds., *The Cultural Nature of Attachment: Contextualizing Relationships and Development*. Cambridge, MA: MIT Press, pp. 231–243.

Sotomayor-Peterson, M., Figueredo, A. J., Christensen, D. H., & Taylor, A. R. (2012). Couples' Cultural Values, Shared Parenting, and Family Emotional Climate within Mexican American Families. *Family Process*, 51(2), 218–233.

Spivak, G. C. (1988). Can the Subaltern Speak? In N. Carry & L. Grossberg, eds., *Marxism and the Interpretation of Culture*. Urbana-Champaign: University of Illinois Press, pp. 271–313.

Stafford, C. (1995). *The Roads of Chinese Childhood: Learning and Identification in Angang*. Cambridge: Cambridge University Press.

Super, C. M., & Harkness, S. (1986). The Developmental Niche: A Conceptualization at the Interface of Child and Culture. *International Journal of Behavioral Development*, 9(4), 545–569.

Therien, J. (2010). Beyond the North–South Divide: The Two Tales of World Poverty. *Third World Quarterly*, 20(4), 723–742. https://doi.org/10.1080/01436599913523.

Tierney, R. K., & Ohnuki-Tierney, E. (2012). Anthropology of Food. In J. M. Pilcher, ed., *The Oxford Handbook of Food History*. Oxford: Oxford University Press, pp. 117–134.

Van der Horst, F. C. (2011). *John Bowlby – From Psychoanalysis to Ethology: Unravelling the Roots of Attachment Theory*. Hoboken, NJ: John Wiley & Sons.

Van der Horst, F. C., LeRoy, H. A., & Van der Veer, R. (2008). "When Strangers Meet": John Bowlby and Harry Harlow on Attachment Behavior. *Integrative Psychological and Behavioral Science*, 42, 370–388.

Van Esterik, P. (2002). Contemporary Trends in Infant Feeding Research. *Annual Review of Anthropology*, 31, 257–278.

Vazir, S., Engle, P., Balakrishna, N. et al. (2013). Cluster-Randomized Trial on Complementary and Responsive Feeding Education to Caregivers Found Improved Dietary Intake, Growth and Development among Rural Indian Toddlers. *Maternal and Child Nutrition*, 9(1), 99–117.

Vicedo, M. (2014). *The Nature and Nurture of Love from Imprinting to Attachment in Cold War America*. Chicago, IL: Chicago University Press.

Viveiros de Castro, E. (1998). Cosmological Deixis and Amerindian Perspectivism. *Journal of the Royal Anthropological Institute N.S.*, 4(3), 469–488.

von Poser, A. (2013). *Foodways and Empathy: Relatedness in a Ramu River Society, Papua New Guinea*. New York: Berghahn Books.

Wacquant, L. (2022). *The Invention of the "Underclass": A Study in the Politics of Knowledge*. New York: Wiley.

Whiting, J., & Whiting, B. (1975). *Children of Six Cultures: A Psychocultural Analysis*. Cambridge, MA: Harvard University Press.

WHO (2009). *Infant and Young Child Feeding: Model Chapter for Textbooks for Medical Students and Allied Health Professionals*. Geneva: World Health Organization.

WHO & UNICEF (2006). *Infant and Young Child Feeding Counseling: An Integrated Course. Trainer's Guide*. Geneva: World Health Organization.

WHO & UNICEF (2012a). *Care for Child Development Package: Facilitator Notes*. www.unicef.org/media/91186/file/5-CCD-Facilitator-Notes.pdf.

WHO & UNICEF (2012b). *Care for Child Development Package: Improving the Care of Young Children*. www.who.int/publications/i/item/9789241548403

WHO, UNICEF, & World Bank Group (2018). *Executive Summary. Nurturing Care for Early Childhood Development: A Framework for Helping Children Survive and Thrive to Transform Health and Human Potential*. Geneva: World Health Organization.

Yu, G.-H. (1991). Ritual, Society, and Culture among the Yami. PhD dissertation, University of Michigan.

Yu, G.-H., & Dong, S.-Y. (1998). 台灣原住民史:雅美族史篇 [*Historiography of Taiwanese Indigenous People: The Yami*]. Nantou: Taiwan Historica.

Zhou, N., Cheah, C. S. L., Van Hook, J., Thompson, D. A., & Jones, S. S. (2015). A Cultural Understanding of Chinese Immigrant Mothers' Feeding Practices: A Qualitative Study. *Appetite*, 87, 160–167.

Acknowledgements

The idea for this Element grew out of a panel on "Feeding and the Formation of Social Relationships during Childhood" at the first online conference of the European Network for Psychological Anthropology (ENPA), which was hosted at the University of Helsinki in June 2021 and organized by Leberecht Funk and Gabriel Scheidecker. The panel included papers from Aglaia Chatjouli and Francesca Mezzenzana; their participation in this early stage was important to developing the ideas in this Element. We are especially indebted to the research participants in each of our field sites. This publication was financed in part by the open access fund for monographs and edited volumes of the Free University of Berlin.

About the Authors

Bambi L. Chapin is an associate professor of anthropology at the University of Maryland, Baltimore County, USA. Chapin wrote the ethnographic section about feeding practices in Sri Lanka (Section 4) based on her ongoing ethnographic research with Sinhala families since 1999. She also contributed considerably to the introductory Section 1, contributed to the revision of all other sections, and took a leading role in editing the Element.

Nandita Chaudhary is an independent scholar living in India, following a teaching and research career at the University of Delhi, India. She now runs a blog and actively publishes and lectures in the field of cultural psychology, child development, and family studies both in India and abroad. Chaudhary took the lead on the concluding section (Section 8), guided the Element from the start with her long-time experience and insights, and contributed to the revision and editing of all sections.

Christine El Ouardani is an associate professor in the Department of Human Development at California State University, Long Beach, USA. El Ourdani wrote the ethnographic section about villagers in rural Morocco (Section 2) based on her research there examining the daily lives of children in light of the increasing presence of state and global development, educational, and medical institutions. She also contributed considerably to Section 1 and contributed to the revision and editing of all sections.

Leberecht Funk holds a doctoral degree in social and cultural anthropology from the Free University of Berlin, Germany. The ethnographic study in Section 5 is drawn from his fieldwork among the Tao on the Taiwanese island of Lanyu. He initiated and led the Element project, drafted and revised Section 1 and the analysis (Section 7) along with Gabriel Scheidecker, and contributed to the revision and editing of all other sections.

Gabriel Scheidecker is an asistant professor in the Department of Social Anthropology and Cultural Studies at the University of Zurich, Switzerland. Based on his doctoral research about child-rearing and the socialization of emotions in Madagascar, he wrote the ethnographic section about feeding in a pastoralist community in the South of the country (Section 3). He drafted and revised Section 1 and the analysis (Section 7) along with Leberecht Funk, contributed to the concluding section (Section 8), and helped with the revision and editing of all other sections.

Wiebke J. Schmidt, a cultural psychologist at the University of Osnabrück, Germany, conducted her doctoral research in Costa Rica in cooperation with the University of Costa Rica. Together with a local team of researchers, she conducted ethnographic field research in three different cultural groups (urban middle-class San José, rural Guanacaste, and rural Indigenous Bribri) and compared the social networks in which children grow up and the ways in which they develop attachment relationships. Schmidt wrote the ethnographic section about Costa Rica (Section 6), contributed to drafting Section 1 and the analysis (Section 7), contributed to the revision and editing of all sections, and took care of the References.

Cambridge Elements ☰

Psychology and Culture

Kenneth D. Keith

University of San Diego

Kenneth D. Keith is author or editor of more than 160 publications on cross-cultural psychology, quality of life, intellectual disability, and the teaching of psychology. He was the 2017 president of the Society for the Teaching of Psychology.

About the Series

Elements in Psychology and Culture features authoritative surveys and updates on key topics in cultural, cross-cultural, and indigenous psychology. Authors are internationally recognized scholars whose work is at the forefront of their subdisciplines within the realm of psychology and culture.

Cambridge Elements ≡

Psychology and Culture

Elements in the Series

A full series listing is available at: www.cambridge.org/EPAC

Printed in the United States
by Baker & Taylor Publisher Services